T0383405

Mikkeller

The
Unsual
Story

MIK

KEL

By Anders Ryehauge

LER

of an
Unusual
(Beer) Brand

Preface

In April of 2021, I was invited to meet with Mikkeller and Strandberg Publishing. They had decided the time had come to tell the whole story about the Danish brewery—from Mikkel Bjergsø's first dubious attempt to clone beer in his kitchen in Copenhagen and right up to today, when Mikkeller owns bars and restaurants all over the world, has launched more than a thousand beers, and has long since grown too large to be referred to as a "microbrewery."

I wasn't a Mikkeller fan beforehand—nor was I skeptic as such. In fact, as the type who always orders whatever lager happens to be on tap, I'd been standing somewhat passively on the sidelines, watching the domestic beer revolution. New, creative breweries were popping up everywhere, bringing not only beers that were different in both taste and appearance but also new types of bars and restaurants to the cityscape—even festivals and running clubs.

Although Mikkeller was, quite obviously, at the forefront of this movement, I'd never really understood what it was all about. So, when I was asked if I wanted to write the book, I saw it as an opportunity not only to try to understand what made Mikkeller so popular, but also to try to understand a piece of modern cultural history.

In late spring of 2021, Mikkel Bjergsø and I met for the first time at Mikkeller's headquarters in the Vesterbro neighborhood in Copenhagen. After that, I accompanied him several times around the country when he had to do something—usually hold a meeting about a potential new project—but also several times outside the country's borders, with a portable recorder in my hand.

Therefore, I was also present when Mikkeller suddenly encountered the most turbulent time in the company's history, one involving both internal and external challenges. Naturally, this new chapter had to be included in the great narrative.

All things considered, I realized that Mikkeller had found itself in an interesting position. After many years of continuous growth, the company was standing on the threshold of a new era, one filled with both opportunities and challenges. Therefore, it seemed only natural that now was the time to write the definitive retrospective on the first (almost) twenty years in the brewery's diverse history.

Whether you're an inveterate fan or, maybe like me, you're simply curious about it all, I hope that the book provides insight into one of the most unique Danish entrepreneurial adventures of recent times and the man behind it.

– Anders Ryehauge

INTRO DUCTION

It's late August of 2021, and all over the streets of Stockholm, people are strolling around in shorts and skirts. The heat from the baking summer sun makes their foreheads glisten. They saunter in and out of cafés and shopping centers and past the city's green parks, where children swing and play soccer. Some head down an otherwise quiet side street in Södermalm, where the inside of Mikkeller's bar is packed. From the bar's many wooden benches, men's and women's voices rise to the ceiling, where they mix with steam from sweaty runners trying to catch their breath with a cold draft beer in their hands.

The bar's owners have arranged a meet-and-greet to celebrate the opening of a new Mikkeller in the Swedish capital. Mikkel Bjergsø, the now former CEO Kenneth Madsen, and American investor Jesse Du Bey are present, along with a large group of employees from the ever-growing microbrewery's headquarters. Before that, Mikkeller Running Club's Stockholm chapter held a race, where they covered almost four kilometers from the first bar in Norrmalm to here. A bright red sign featuring the text "Söder" and the iconic characters Henry & Sally, who've become synonymous with Mikkeller, hangs in front of the red brick wall.

Mikkel Bjergsø is the focus of events this early Saturday afternoon—not of his own volition but because it's inevitable when you've spearheaded a brand that's created an established fan base on the other side of the Sound separating Denmark and Sweden. Several of the guests have traveled from other cities in Sweden, and a few even from Norway, to be here on this day.

At one point, when he has a rare moment of quiet, Bjergsø whispers in his understated, sarcastic manner: "Why don't we go to a real pub instead?"

The New York Times once described Bjergsø as "tall and taciturn, with a solemn bearing that can make him appear extremely bored even when he's in good spirits." That trait has been observed frequently since then, and he's often described as quiet and simply "uninterested." Pernille Pang, the mother of his children and his former partner for many years, has commented that some of her friends found him arrogant when the couple first started seeing each other.

The truth is, however, that he's most comfortable out of the spotlight. He's not particularly fond of attention, even the positive kind, and becomes easily embarrassed. Although he could run around to receptions and bar and restaurant openings all year long—he certainly gets enough invitations—he'd rather not, because he doesn't really enjoy them. Introverted and shy by nature, he has often insisted that he'd prefer if people showed more interest in his beer than in him as a person. At the opening of Mikkeller's first bar in Tokyo, about a thousand people showed up, all of whom wanted to see "the giraffe"—that is, the Danish microbrewer. Eventually it all became too much for him, so he ran off and hid in a corner wine bar, one dark enough that no one could spot him. That way, he could avoid having his picture taken or signing any more autographs.

It's not that Mikkel Bjergsø hates speaking to other people. On the contrary, for years he has sought out collaborations of almost any kind: any conversation with a concrete purpose means something to him. On the other hand, he can't abide small-talk—he has no desire to make idle chatter with people he doesn't even know. Since he's not one to play-act, he often ends up simply saying nothing, which seems to confirm the general impression that he's arrogant.

It doesn't help that he often looks so serious, thanks to his usually somber facial expression. Conversely, that characteristic supports the narrative about him and the Danish microbrewery, which for many years has been almost one and the same. In 2014, the Danish business newspaper *Børsen* described him as

the antithesis of the jovial fat man from the old Tuborg Beer poster, the one who wipes sweat off his neck with his handkerchief. Instead, the newspaper found Bjergsø "cool" and "a hit in hipster circles."

Paradoxically, Bjergsø has never hidden the fact that he has an ambivalent relationship with beer nerds. Although he's the very one who has created bars that serve as magnets for those aficionados, his ambition right from the start has been to open the beer world up to everyone. Still, when you've constantly tried to push the limits of what's possible, and when you've become possibly the most prominent Dane ever in the beer industry—with the exception of Carlsberg founder J.P. Jacobsen—how could you not become some kind of icon? Of course, the incessant stories about the fierce rivalry with his twin brother,

Mikkel Bjergsø has never really craved attention—but Mikkeller's ever-growing reputation has made it unavoidable.

with whom he has not spoken in more than ten years, have only helped to reinforce the myth. Today, legions of fans—from Japan to Russia to the US—can show off tattoos from the Danish craft brewery. In Canada and Singapore, some fans have even christened their child "Mikkeller." So, even though Bjergsø prefers his privacy, there's no way around the global attention.

One early summer day in 2022, Mikkel Bjergsø is sitting in the kitchen of his apartment on the border between the Frederiksberg and Vesterbro sections of Copenhagen. From the open door to the sun-drenched roof terrace, he can hear the sound of children playing in a nearby schoolyard. The day before, he returned home from Japan, where Mikkeller has several bars in Tokyo's Shibuya district. He'd also recently been on a long trip in Florida, where he talked to many different brewers and beer nerds. To his great satisfaction, many people told him that they still regarded the Danish microbrewery as an inspiration.

"Many of the breweries that started at the same time we did are irrelevant today," he says. "Several of them are doing well enough in terms of earnings, but nobody views them as an inspiration anymore. They still make beer and make money, but they don't *contribute* anything. That being said, you also have to get up early in the morning these days to remain relevant—because tomorrow a new brewery will pop up farther down the street, one people find more interesting. You can be the most hyped place in the world one day and then completely irrelevant tomorrow."

When Bjergsø began experimenting in his kitchen twenty years ago—solely because he wanted to copy his favorite beer so he could save money—he never expected he'd be starting a new career. He was actually a schoolteacher, and even after founding Mikkeller a few years later, his intention was to continue teaching. That was not to be, however, as everyone now knows; still, his strange background in the beer industry wound up benefiting him anyway. What started as a hobby turned into a microbrewery, which then turned into several bars and restaurants, a running club, and a festival with some ten thousand participants. Not to mention myriad other projects, both big and small.

"If you attend Copenhagen Business School, you learn how to run a company. If you go to the Scandinavian School of Brewing, you learn how to brew. In both cases, much of the teaching is about what not to do. I've met many brewers who've said you can't put as much hops in as I have, because it says so in the books. But I haven't read them. Just as I've never read that when you start a business you *have* to do well in your home country first before you move outside the country's borders. So I started out in the world. Because I had no idea what the limitations were, I wasn't restricted by them either. I just did what I thought was fun—what I was interested in," he says.

Over the last twenty years, Bjergsø has rarely stopped to reflect on what he has actually achieved. He's almost always focused on moving on to the next goal. Once in a while it hits him anyway—the effect he's had on that part of the world—and he feels a tinge of pride somewhere deep inside.

"I never expected to get this far—to have an entire industry view me as someone who has made a big difference. After all, you can't plan something like this. I actually don't see myself at all as someone whose intent was to create something like this. Sometimes I wonder how the hell I got here."

I

KITCHEN EXPERIMENTS

In 1994, Mikkel Bjergsø found himself in the US Midwest, in the Sunflower State of Kansas, to be exact. Once he'd started middle-distance running as an eleven-year-old in Denmark, things picked up speed for him. Training and running filled his life. Later, when his classmates started turning their attention toward drinking, he stayed on the straight and narrow. He was extremely dedicated, often training twelve times a week and winning several youth championships, including one for the Danish track and field club Sparta. That win provided numerous opportunities, and as a nineteen-year-old he was invited to Kansas State in the United States on a scholarship. He became part of the university's athletics team, and that same year he won the award as "Outstanding Wildcat Freshman."

In addition to running, Bjergsø studied chemistry and physics at college. In his spare time, he sat in his room on campus listening to Nirvana and Pearl Jam, and he cultivated a newfound interest in furniture design. He'd been fascinated by iconic American diner culture, which had led him to a more general interest in colorful plastic furniture—which would later lead him to the Dane Verner Panton, whose designs he diligently collected (and whom he still considers the greatest of them all).

However, that wasn't the only revelation to emerge from his time in the United States. While there, he had his first encounter with microbrewing. Bjergsø—who'd lived an almost ascetic youthful life until then—could no longer avoid imbibing when his new American acquaintances decided to live it up now and then. Although it was illegal to drink alcohol because he was under twenty-one, he still took a few dives into otherwise unknown waters. Naturally, he tasted Budweiser, the most widely drunk American beer, and Coors Light, which was also very popular, but at one point he got hold of a bottle of Dead Guy Ale from Rogue. The dark bottle from the Oregon-based brewery had a skeleton in the fetal position as a sticker. The taste made a lasting impression on the young Dane, who thought, "So this is how beer could taste …"

Not long after his stay in the Midwest, Bjergsø returned to the US, this time spending half a year in Alabama on a new scholarship. While living in the Bible belt, he discovered rednecks and Baptists—and he gained insight into the observance of Jim Crow laws and racial segregation (though legally abolished, they still had a foothold in certain Southern societies). It was all foreign to him, having grown up in Kokkedal, north of Copenhagen, yet he had consciously sought it out, first among cowboys in Kansas and now in Alabama. Unlike so many others who went to California or Florida in search of Edenic beaches, he wanted to experience "the real United States."

"It was really exciting, although I also saw a lot of crap," he comments. "In Alabama, whites and blacks lived in totally separate areas. You were told point blank that you weren't supposed to go into the black areas, and if you drove through black neighborhoods anyway, you could plainly see the difference. Almost all the houses were dilapidated, with bullet holes in their walls. It was really low class—and it was solely because they didn't have the same opportunities. I was not used to that in Denmark, so it was pretty wild to experience."

During his time in Alabama, Bjergsø lived at a Christian university, where alcohol use was strictly forbidden and you were fined if you violated it (which he did). He lived in a house on campus with four other runners from the team, all Americans, and during one of their countless parties, which they held anyway, their coach caught them red-handed. It resulted in both a reprimand and a fine for all five of them. Because Bjergsø was the team's star, however, he told the coach: "If you don't delete those fines, I'm going home to Denmark." The fines were lifted.

DARREN WHITLEY/Collegian

Mikkel Bjergso races through the course at Warner Park. Bjergso finished in 36th place, while racing in his first ever Big Eight Championships. Overall, the men's team finished in 7th place. Geoff Delahanty captured the high finish for the Cats, with a 30th place finish.

runner, senior Billy Wuggazer, experienced side cramps, which caused him to run a sub-par race.

"Billy ran really bad because he stitched up," Drake said. "If he would have been where he's capable of placing, we would have accomplished our goal of placing sixth."

The ailing Wuggazer finished in 38th position behind teammates junior Geoff Delahanty in 30th and freshman Mikkel Bjergso in 36th.

Delahanty said although he was the highest finisher for the Cats, he was still not altogether pleased with his showing.

"People have been telling me that I ran a good race," Delahanty said. "It was probably the best finish in a race that I've had, but it's still not even close to as good as I can run.

"I might have gotten a little overzealous and just run a little too quick sometimes."

Delahanty said if Wuggazer and himself had run to their potential, the outcome of the race would have been much different.

"Billy could have been top 10 easy, and I could have been top 15, if we would have run like we've been in practice," Wuggazer said.

Iowa State dominated the meet with only 29 points, giving them the championship.

Wuggazer said the overall place of the team doesn't matter as much as giving the younger runners some experience.

"Since we have a lot of freshmen and sophomores right now, it's not really that important right now," Wuggazer said. "As long as they get to know how the competition is and observe, then they'll be fine."

Entering the NCAA District V Championships, Drake said he has a completely different outlook for his two teams.

Drake said he is hoping to take the women's team to the NCAA Championships.

"For the next two weeks, we'll focus on sharpening. We'll lower the mileage some and maybe raise the intensity a little," Drake said.

In the men's division, Drake said he isn't really worried about the team's outcome.

"What we're really going to focus on is getting Billy to nationals and have Jeff and Mikkel running well," Drake said. "We're going to take a weakened team to districts."

In 1994, Mikkel Bjergsø was on a running scholarship at Kansas State University. This photo was taken for a local newspaper during a race.

In time Bjergsø realized that he'd never be the fastest runner. He really had trouble keeping up with the Kenyan runners. It was no longer enough simply to *want* the most, as it had been at home, so he gradually lost motivation. Eventually he dropped out and moved back to Denmark in 1997.

In Denmark, he wanted to be a completely ordinary student. He was twenty-two years old, yet he'd never really had any wild youth. He had a fine youth—that wasn't the problem—and he'd traveled a lot, participated in world championships, and tried a little of everything. Still, he felt that he had missed *something*.

Bjergsø moved into his own apartment on the border between Frederiksberg and Vesterbro and started studying at Frederiksberg Teachers' College. He really wanted to study at Blågårds Teachers' College, but his twin brother Jeppe had already started there—and neither of them wanted to subject himself to the endless comparisons. During his teacher training at Frederiksberg, the beer immediately started to flow. He and his new-found friends often hung out at Enghave Plads in Copenhagen, where they drank far into the night, sometimes bathing in the fountain in the bright morning hours.

It didn't really matter *what* they drank, as long as they got enough of it. Throughout most of his first year, Bjergsø drank only Bear Beer, the beer that had the highest alcohol content for your money. Otherwise, they mostly drank Carlsberg, and later the American Miller High Life when it surfaced as one of the first foreign beers in Denmark. At the time, he didn't really notice how bad it actually tasted, because there was nothing to compare it to.

In the late 1990s, Bjergsø started to frequent Oonas, a bar in Copenhagen. At this time there weren't really any bars in Denmark that carried foreign beers—and there were no microbreweries to be found. In fact, there were only a few breweries in all of Denmark,
primarily the large ones: Carlsberg, Royal, and Harboe. At Oonas, though, you could get foreign beer. You could even buy a bucket filled with ice and ten special beers for 150 crowns (about $25). That option quickly became a tradition among Bjergsø's group of friends—so much so that bartenders started calling them "the bucket boys" and quickly placed a new bucket in front of them as soon as they walked in the door.

Seen in retrospect, what Oonas had to offer really wasn't that wild: they had beers like Chimay and Hoegaarden.

"It sounds crazy today, because Hoegaarden is owned by one of the world's largest breweries," says Bjergsø, "but back then it felt kind of special. It was the same when Carlsberg during those years made Carls Hvede—it was wildly exotic to be able to get a wheat beer."

He started to realize that a whole universe of beer existed beyond Denmark's borders. Eventually, Oonas hired him. One day one of the owners asked, "Since you're here all the time anyway, do you want to work here?" He took a job as a bartender and waiter—although he never really got paid any salary because he drank it all away. Later he also became a buyer for the bar, which put him in charge of selecting beers. That's how he became aware of beer from Germany, Belgium, and the Czech Republic, beers that were completely different experiences to drink than what he had previously known.

At the same time, a quiet revolution in beer drinking was happening in Denmark. Whereas Carlsberg had previously dominated everything, small breweries were suddenly springing up here and there. In 1998, the association of Danish Beer Enthusiasts, founded at the pub Carlsens Kvarter in Odense, helped to spread an interest that had mostly been non-existent in Denmark. Mikkel Bjergsø also became a member, although his commitment consisted mostly of reading the members' magazine when it showed up in his mailbox.

"To me, they've always been some old men who enjoy buying whatever beer was on sale at the grocery store," he observes. "Still, I have to acknowledge that they've done something good in creating awareness for beers beyond the most well-known."

In the years that followed, smaller lodges of beer nerds began to spring up around the country—and in 2000, Bjergsø even joined a beer club started by his twin brother Jeppe Jarnit-Bjergsø. The club was named "BØF," an abbreviation for the Danish "Bryg den Øl Foreningen" (Brew that Beer Society). Although the name might suggest so, the club had nothing to do with brewing. The name had arisen because one of its members, Myles, who was South African, despite his otherwise impressive Danish, had a habit of reversing the word order in some of his sentences. When at one point he was going to a christening, for example, he called it "baptize that child." Thus, the way was paved for the group of friends to humor themselves by teasing Myles, especially with the name "Brew that Beer Society."

The members of BØF consisted mostly of Mikkel and Jeppe Bjergsø's circles of friends from college. At most, there were twenty members—they even had their own membership magazine. Because childhood friend and running mate Kristian Keller was a trained journalist, he was responsible for the magazine's startup. It featured reviews of different beers, reports from various trips, and short interviews with fellow members. Most of all, they met regularly and drank beer from interesting breweries, and then fervently discussed their opinions. Blind tastings quickly became a regular custom. Among other things, they crowned the Christmas Beer of the Year (a seasoned beer brewed especially for the holiday). Each member had to bring one Christmas beer, wrapped in silver paper, which they each tasted, graded based on different criteria, and finally ranked to determine a winner.

"What came out tasted kind of like beer—you could imagine it was beer—but it was really nothing more than fermented syrup."

– Mikkel Bjergsø

At other times, they'd vote for the Danish Beer of the Year or Imported Beer of the Year.

From time to time, they went on bus trips to breweries in both Denmark and Germany with the sole purpose of buying new exciting beverages to take home. For example, they went to Hillerød, north of Copenhagen, to visit Brøckhouse, one of the first microbreweries in Denmark that managed to create a name for itself. At that time, according to the members of BØF, Brøckhouse made some of the most interesting beers in Denmark.

It was one thing to finance their alcohol intake when they could drink Bear Beer for four crowns a bottle, but it was another now that interest in microbreweries had increased—along with the price. In 2003, Mikkel Bjergsø and Kristian Keller decided they'd try to clone the beers they particularly liked. The two friends had known each other since their younger days when both were elite runners. Keller, who lived in Rønne on the island of Bornholm, ran in the Bornholm running club Viking. Therefore, whenever Mikkel and Jeppe were at a training camp on the rocky island, they would stay at Keller's, and conversely, the Bornholm resident always found shelter with the twins when he was at track meets on Zealand.

At first, they merely experimented in the kitchen of Bjergsø's apartment in Vesterbro. Both beer aficionados had become more interested in understanding the purely technical aspect behind making the beers they liked. In particular, they loved the IPA—an India Pale Ale that Brøckhouse had released the year before. "That one was the whole reason I started brewing myself, because I wanted to make a clone of it," he admits.

Initially, they borrowed some books from the library and bought a 20-liter pot from the Danish supermarket Føtex and a relatively primitive beer kit with malt extract, which had already been hopped with a small packet of dry yeast on top, from the drug store Matas.

Bjergsø had found the books. Although the Internet was expanding at that time, virtually no material on beer-brewing existed. At the library, on the other hand, they found books in English written by, among others, Charlie Papazian: the "godfather" of homebrewing had already established himself in the US as a professional homebrewer with the publication of his book *The Complete Joy of Homebrewing*.

Bjergsø and Keller soon realized, however, that even Papazian's teachings couldn't help that beer kit from Matas.

"It was the kind of thing where you just had to add water and syrup," recalls Bjergsø. "You didn't actually have to do anything yourself. We tried the first five brews. What came out tasted kind of like beer—you could imagine that it was beer—but in reality, it was just some kind of fermented syrup. That wasn't why we'd started in the first place. I wanted to make beer like Brøckhouse, but this stuff came no way near."

From here, the experimenting homebrewers soon gained ground. At first, they bought different malt extracts and ingredients to color the beer with, but it still didn't taste like what the breweries made. There was too much syrup. Instead, they switched to all grain, like the professionals; you buy ingredients such as hops and malt, and grind the latter yourself. They were able to order from Brygladen, a webshop in Vejle, that offered homebrewing materials—probably the only place in the country that carried the necessary goods.

At about the same time, the first official Danish homebrewing association started, with

Along with his friends, Bjergsø started the beer club BØF, where they also produced their own membership magazine, *The Beer Nut*. This edition is from October 2003.

regular meetings where they shared recipes with each other. Mikkel Bjergsø and Kristian Keller showed up to meet the other more or less hopeful homebrewers. At the request of the two friends, one of the members opened a homebrew shop called Maltbazaren in Copenhagen shortly thereafter, which made certain things easier.

Mikkel Bjergsø's apartment in Vesterbro was soon transformed into a kind of laboratory filled with strange fumes, large pots, and plastic containers. Even though they had to throw out their first attempts, they still came closer to a brew resembling the real thing. As a trained schoolteacher in chemistry and physics, Bjergsø had some prior understanding of the chemical processes.

"When brewing beer, there's a lot of chemistry in the molecules that are converted. For example, we used iodine to see if they were converted properly. If you don't know much about chemistry, it might sound a bit abstract—but because I understood the process, I could change it," he explains.

Bjergsø and Keller's actual mission, however, was to try to clone their favorite beer, the famous IPA from Brøckhouse. That was the real purpose of their homebrewing adventure. Therefore, they wrote to the brewer in Hillerød and inquired about the ingredients. Although they weren't given exact ratios of the different hops and malts, they could roughly figure out what ingredients to use. So, they went ahead with their own beer, which they christened, with a subtle tip of the hat, "Brauhaus IPA."

"We made several versions, constantly trying to change it a little," he says. "We flavored it with various ingredients, trying to figure out how much they used of each one. Once we'd made a beer, we compared it to the original. If it was too bitter, we had to cut down the bitter hops; if it was too dark, we had to remove some of the malt that gave it color; and if it was too sweet, we could

change malt types or lower the liquid temperature. There were different things we could do to try to hit the mark."

Kristian Keller lived on the other side of the courtyard in the same apartment complex, so he could hop over quickly when it was time for another brew. And that was often the case. The numerous ingredients were stored in both the apartment and one of the basement rooms.

Their building superintendent Poul-Erik, a member of the Danish Beer Enthusiasts, became so excited that someone was brewing beer on the property that he gave them a larger basement room. Whenever something broke and needed to be fixed—which was often—he was always ready with a helping hand. Bjergsø and Keller had started with a 20-liter pot, but now they had invested in a 150-liter one, which they tried to heat by lighting all four burners on the glass-ceramic stovetop at the same time. From time to time, the plate overheated and burned completely, and then they had to call Poul-Erik again. He'd rip up the plate and fix it, so they could continue brewing on it.

After about ten attempts in the home kitchen, their own brew tasted, to the best of their knowledge, exactly like the beer that came from the North Zealand brewery. After almost half a year, they had actually done what they set out to do.

For Mikkel Bjergsø, it had become his whole life: "I loved brewing—I loved the various processes. There was so much to do on brewing day. There were specific routines for how to clean properly, prepare the cooler, sparge hot water. It really was a great time."

On the other hand, Bjergsø's girlfriend Pernille Pang, who also lived in the apartment, was less enthused. Not that she was complaining all the time—she just couldn't hide the fact that she found it all to be too much. At the time, she was an intern at the Danish newspaper *Politiken*. When she'd come home after

Kristian Keller crushes malt in the cellar under Mikkel Bjergsø's apartment in Mikkeller's earliest days.

long days of tight deadlines and needed to relax, she'd find the two ambitious homebrewers in full swing. By the time she reached the stairwell, it already smelled of hops. Inside, the apartment was all steamed up. Because they used such a large pot, liters of moisture would evaporate, creating a dark liquid that ran down the walls. All the clothes and furniture in the apartment eventually reeked of malt and hops. Large 120-liter plastic buckets were strewn all over the place, because the two friends brewed a new batch almost every weekend. Since it took about four weeks to ferment, the number of plastic buckets piled up quickly. They were bubbling all the time, especially at night when the couple was trying to sleep. *Plop, plop, plop.*

Even though Pernille Pang often found it all quite annoying, she had to admit that it

At first, Mikkel Bjergsø and Kristian Keller attempted to clone beer. Afterwards, they began to craft their own. Pictured are some of the first bottles with their own home brew.

was fun—and more often than not she ended up on the sidelines. She and Bjergsø had gotten to know each other a few years earlier. He was having a party in his apartment one evening, and a friend who attended the teachers' college with him asked if she could come over. Soon, she met the whole gang, which included Mikkel's twin brother Jeppe, Kristian Keller, and Søren Runge, who today is responsible for Mikkeller Running Club.

In addition to training as a journalist, Pernille Pang played music in her own band Tiger Baby, which she joined in 1998. She released her first album with the band in 2004. They enjoyed moderate success on the Danish indie scene with their electronic indie pop and managed to be named "Unavoidable This Week" on the Danish radio station P3. The band played concerts at such Copenhagen venues as Stengade 30, VEGA, and RUST and performed at various venues in Germany, New York, and Indonesia. In Indonesia, for slightly obscure reasons, they became a hit after one of their songs appeared on the soundtrack to an MTV-produced film in the Southeast Asian country. Because music was an integral part of her identity, her curiosity was immediately aroused when, at that party in Bjergsø's apartment, she spotted the thin CD shelf that surrounded the entire living room; it was packed with bootlegs and rare live recordings. She knew she had found someone as nerdy as she was when it came to music.

Before long they started dating. They were both in their twenties, a couple of real indie kids constantly listening to music, talking about music, and going to concerts. They didn't have a care in the world. At that time, Mikkel Bjergsø was still studying to become a teacher. Every Thursday to Saturday, he went to Ideal Bar or VEGA with his crew and drank a lot of beer. He spent most of the rest of the week lying down. He couldn't care less about his studies and he seemed quite lazy. Therefore, Pang had no idea that her boyfriend would one day make it big. On the other hand, she envied his ability to show up to his oral exams without having read anything and still pull it off in a convincing manner. Conversely, she was totally conscientious, reading everything that needed to be read, yet still getting nervous when she had to give a presentation.

Along with his interest in music, she initially fell for his laid-back attitude as well. Sometimes people confused it for arrogance—but those who really knew him knew that, mostly, he was introverted and had an informal manner. At the same time, he was a bit rebellious by nature. He hated when things had to be a certain way, which meant that he despised traditions—especially Christmas. Pernille Pang quickly christened him "Ebenezer Scrooge" (after the malicious Christmas-loathing businessman from *A Christmas Carol*). One year, shortly before he would become a father for the first time, Bjergsø decided to celebrate Christmas at Christiania by handing out food to the homeless, something his mother-in-law found rather odd. Pernille was more accepting: she had learned early on that once he made his mind up, there was nothing you could do. You had to just let him do it.

Mikkel Bjergsø never did anything halfheartedly. Pernille could see this when at one point he pushed aside his interest in music for a new all-consuming interest in design. He'd cultivated it sporadically since he first saw midcentury design in the US—but now he threw himself full-force into Danish design, trying to learn everything there was to know about it in record time. He was especially taken with Verner Panton, who in the 1960s was one of the most influential designers in Europe; while studying at the teachers' college, Bjergsø made quite a lucrative business for himself traveling to auctions and buying up designs, which he then sold. At one point, he found a Panton lamp, that he subsequently sold to a Japanese buyer on eBay for almost ten times the price.

Afterward, Bjergsø became obsessed with beer. From the sidelines, Pernille watched as his interest grew and took hold. Initially, she was really bored when his friends came over, sitting there for hours talking about beer. In time, she started to enjoy it, especially once he also started doing his own brewing—and sometimes she was even able to help. For example, she sewed little Santa hats to sit on top of the bottle caps when they made a Christmas beer at one point. For their first beer festival, she crafted Mikkeller merchandise with a stencil that Kristian Keller had made, and which she then printed on various T-shirts.

At the same time that Mikkel Bjergsø started homebrewing on weekends, in 2003, he also started teaching at Det Frie Gymnasium, a private school in Copenhagen. Although he should have graduated in 2001, he postponed his last exam so that he could receive an educational grant for one more year while still working as a bartender at Oonas. He was also emptying dead people's estates for a shop in Copenhagen's Østerbro section before finally graduating in 2002. During his first year as a graduate, he held various part-time positions before finally becoming a full-time school-teacher—but he had also become a part-time homebrewer. Even though the original mission was simply to clone their favorite beer from Brøckhouse, it didn't stop there. With the same dedication as an elite runner in his youth, he began training himself for microbrewery. He wanted to learn all about the ingredients, understand how the myriad variations of hops tasted, and why malt could be so different.

At that time, Ølbaren, the first real beer bar in Copenhagen, had opened in the city's hip Nørrebro section, and in 2001 Plan B also opened on Frederiksborggade in the Inner City.

"I remember it was absolutely wild at the time, because there were bars with all sorts of different kinds of beer. Otherwise, you could only find pubs and Irish pubs with Carlsberg, Royal, and Guinness," he recalls.

At the same time, the Danish microbrewery scene was gaining momentum. In 2005 it suddenly exploded with 35 microbreweries opening in Denmark in a single year. Most of them were very small and local—you still couldn't find anything special in the supermarkets—but something was definitely brewing. You could see it in the comments on the website RateBeer, the large, virtual international watering hole for beer nerds.

"For some reason it was really hardcore in Denmark," says Bjergsø. "I think half of those in the top ten with the most reviews were Danes. It became a community where people met and nerded out about beers they'd procured from all over the world. I was also invited to such a tasting, and there you really encountered all sorts of strange things."

The big turning point for Bjergsø came, however, when he got the opportunity to taste beer from some of the new American microbreweries, such as Stone Brewing and AleSmith from San Diego in California and 3 Floyds Brewing from Indiana. Their selection included IPAs, Double IPAs, and Imperial Stouts—wild and extreme beers that differed from anything he had ever tried. It was a completely different experience than drinking Brøckhouse's IPA.

"IPA was originally an English style of beer, but American versions had started to appear, which basically meant that there would be more of all of it. They were much wilder—it involved trying everything," explains Bjergsø.

It had taken Mikkel Bjergsø half a year to complete his original mission of cloning Brøckhouse. Now, it was clearly time for the next step: there were much wilder and more interesting beers to be found on the market.

"I could see that they were creating something wilder than what I'd experienced at home in Denmark, and I wanted to show that to people who were into beer. I wanted to show what could be done in the United States."

A batch of homebrew fermenting in Mikkel Bjergsø's former home. During the approximately four weeks it took to ferment, they heard constant bubbling coming from the plastic buckets scattered around the apartment.

II

GIGAN
TIC
HOP
SOCKS

After cloning their first beers, Mikkel Bjergsø and Kristian Keller were ready to create one of their very own—and that meant experimenting. They now knew how to make an IPA, so it wasn't that difficult to make one that was even wilder. To put it bluntly, that meant stuffing in more hops—and then freestyling from there.

"When people ask about getting started brewing at home, my best advice is always to take a beer you love and try to clone it. That way you learn an insane amount about the processes. Once you know what happens if you raise the mash temperature, or what difference it makes when you add the hops, then it's like cooking. And then you can start making your own decisions. Because it takes six to eight weeks before you sit down with the finished bottle, many people would rather try everything possible along the way. They make an IPA the first week, a stout the week after that, and then a wheat beer—but you don't learn shit by doing that. You never get down to business and understand what's really going on," says Bjergsø.

For the two friends, the whole process of cloning beer from Brøckhouse had in no way been a complete triumph. They'd learned a lot along the way, including the importance of cleaning when brewing beer. Therefore, they started to hold their breath whenever they opened the fermentation bucket to transfer the beer, thus minimizing the risk of spreading bacteria.

"We were pretty careful with everything. If you're impatient and just want to get it over with, you'll make more mistakes. Maybe we were a little obsessive, but we felt that we might as well do it all as cleanly as possible. That way we didn't have as many big fuck-ups as we probably could have had. However, you can't completely avoid infections. Bacteria can get into the chiller or the airlock—and before you know it, things have gone wrong," he observes.

Their efforts had been pure trial and error. On the other hand, they gradually —instinctively—came to understand almost all the processes.

"Once you've done it before," explains Bjergsø, "you can roughly figure out when different things happen in the process. That allowed us to start making our own recipes, also for other styles of beer. Because once you've learned the processes, you can start experimenting with other ingredients."

Meanwhile, they started garnering increasingly positive reactions to their home brew. It was a real feather in their cap when their copy of Brøckhouse's IPA, in a blind tasting among a large group of beer enthusiasts, was named Denmark's Best Beer in 2005. Yet, even though Bjergsø was naturally happy, he also realized that honors like that only said so much about his abilities. He wanted to be judged by people who didn't even know him. Therefore, he and Keller officially founded their own microbrewery, "Mikkeller," in 2005—the name was a contraction of one's first name and the other's last name.

When Mikkel's twin brother, Jeppe Jarnit-Bjergsø, opened his pub, Ølbaren, in Vesterbro in Copenhagen the same year, he started to sell some of the beers that Mikkel and Kristian were brewing at home in the kitchen. Typically, they produced about a hundred bottles at a time; they received no money for it, but in return they were allowed to take home new and interesting foreign beers. Ølbaren quickly became quite well known in beer circles. When Danish beer nerds wanted to exchange beer with their American counterparts, they'd stop by the shop to find something from a Danish microbrewery that they could send across the Atlantic. Mikkel Bjergsø was determined to have his beer make the trip overseas—then he could read what Americans thought of it on the international beer site RateBeer.

"It's fine when your friends think your beer tastes good—but what about the people who don't even know you? I really wanted to get reactions from people who had no idea

who I was, so I could find out if people actually liked it or if they were just being kind."

During the day, Bjergsø was still teaching at Det Frie Gymnasium in Copenhagen. He loved his job, but deep inside the idea of revolutionizing what he saw as the deadly-dull Danish beer market had also begun to germinate. Unlike American breweries, which were not afraid to break the rules, Danish breweries suffered from a lack of imagination. There were virtually no variations in the beers being crafted, and although new microbreweries opened regularly, in his book most of them were a bit boring.

"Although a lot of microbreweries were opening, most of them were very small. Carlsberg had 97 percent of the market—and it

Mikkel Bjergsø and his twin brother, Jeppe, at Ølbutikken in Copenhagen. Between them is Greg Koch from Stone Brewing Company, a notable figure in the American craft beer world. Stone was the first brewery that Mikkeller—along with another brewery, AleSmith—did a "collab" with back in 2007.

wasn't really a public that went in for specialty beers. So, most of the new breweries made beer that tasted like Carlsberg's," he says.

That wasn't enough for Mikkel Bjergsø. He wanted to push the envelope—and even though he was just a modest homebrewer in an apartment with evaporating dark liquid dripping down the walls, he saw signs that he was on the right track. Several of his beers made their way across the Atlantic, and on RateBeer, he could see increasing interest. A number of beer drinkers wrote that they were impressed that you could make this kind of beer in Denmark.

One of the very first beers that he and Kristian Keller made, a Belgian tripel that was a light but strong and very alcoholic beer, won the silver medal at the Danish Championships in Homebrewing. You submitted beer in different categories, which a judge then tasted, assessed, and rated. Soon after, several silver medals came to the collection, and in 2005 they also won the gold medal in the category "Brown Ale."

Bjergsø also trained to become an official beer judge—one of the very first in Denmark. For the first Danish competitions, they had to rely solely on judges from Sweden: at that time, people could be trained there, but not in Denmark.

"When you evaluate beer, it's not so much about whether it tastes good," explains Bergsø. "Beer is assessed primarily on certain parameters, such as whether there is a defect in the beer, whether it's in the right color spectrum, the right bitterness spectrum, and its percentage of alcohol. There are guidelines within beer in all styles."

Once education in evaluating beer arrived in Denmark—with Swedish teachers—Bjergsø was on the very first team, along with Keller. They became officially trained beer judges who could judge competitions both at home and abroad. Training took place in Copenhagen at a series of weekend courses. You studied for a written exam with technical questions about beer, including "What happens if you raise the mash temperature two degrees?" You had to assess the type, alcohol percentage, and any errors of different beers. Usually, mistakes were deliberately added, which then had to be ascertained.

"It gave me knowledge about beer that I could use later. For example, I can quickly spot any flaws that exist in beer. Very few can, because they don't know what to look for. You might find that the beer tastes strange, but only a few people can figure out why."

Suddenly, Mikkel Bjergsø and Kristian Keller had a major breakthrough when they invented the stout Beer Geek Breakfast. The oat stout was made with the help of a coffee-plunger or French press—which instantly sent the beer world into a state of ecstasy. In 2006, their new creation was named the world's best stout. Mikkeller suddenly found itself 37th best microbrewery out of a total of 5,836 worldwide on RateBeer (even though they were still doing all their brewing at home).

"It was fun to win with something we'd made in a plastic bucket in the kitchen. It was our own invention. We actually made a lot of our equipment ourselves," he says.

Among other things, they used a metal container, which had nothing to do with brewing equipment, and then added a strange tap wrapped in sleeping mats so that it would stay warm. They also kept a chiller that they made with copper pipes standing on the toilet, and they continued to ferment everything in a plastic bucket.

"There isn't a single brewery in the world today that could devise it. Things are always made of stainless steel and conical. So it was pretty cool that we could still make the world's best beer in one category just by standing in our kitchen at home," he says.

The positive ratings on RateBeer created a lot of hype, casting an international spotlight on Mikkeller and serving as an early catalyst for the brewery's success. They still didn't

Mikkeller

Beer Geek Breakfast

Breakfast is the most important meal of the day and to beer geeks, like Mikkeller, a hearty, complex stout is the best way to begin the day. This unique mix of an oat and coffee stout creates an intense, full-bodied beer, which is surprisingly balanced and full of new taste adventures with every sip.

BREWED & BOTTLED BY
MIKKELLER
AT GOURMETBRYGGERIET
ROSKILDE, DENMARK

IMPORTED BY
SHELTON BROTHERS
BELCHERTOWN, MA

IA-OR-VT-CT-MA-ME-DE-
NY-5¢ REF MI-10¢ REF
FL **CA CASH REFUND** OK+

6 08782 66918 9

OATMEAL STOUT BREWED WITH COFFEE   7.5% ALC./VOL.   1 PT 6 FL OZ

Top: the first Beer Geek Breakfast label. Since then, there have been countless variants, such as the one below. Beer Geek Breakfast holds a special place in Mikkeller's history—in many ways it was the beer that kick-started everything.

exist officially, so people around the world were asking: "Who the hell are these people from Denmark making their own beer?" They were producing only a hundred bottles of each beer and brewing only fifty liters of beer at a time when importers suddenly started contacting them.

Shortly thereafter, Bjergsø and Keller announced that they would release their first official beer as a company at the Danish Beer Enthusiasts' festival in May of the same year. That immediately resulted in six different US distributors making inquiries. There had been rumors on the American continent for some time that two Danish homebrewers, experimenting in their kitchen, were behind these famous beers from Mikkeller. Therefore, the

Mikkel Bjergsø and Kristian Keller present Beer Geek Breakfast at the Danish Beer Enthusiasts Beer Festival in the middle of the aughts.

announcement that they were officially releasing the first 2,000 liters of beer immediately aroused interest. Two of the American importers flew straight to Copenhagen in connection with the festival—solely to meet the two Danes, who over the weekend ended up signing a contract with one of them.

Mikkeller suddenly had potential access to a larger audience in the United States—at a time when only a few people outside the most passionate beer circles in Denmark had ever even heard of them. Quite an unusual development, but now that the opportunity had arisen, Bjergsø was determined to run with it.

"It was hard to imagine a Danish microbrewery exporting beer to the US. It had never happened before. Yet I felt like there were five million Danes at home, and everyone drank Carlsberg. If I could start selling to a country with over three hundred million residents, one where at least ten percent drank craft beer, it might provide some completely different opportunities. No matter what business education you pursue, you learn that you must be in control of your home market before you start exporting. But I hadn't been educated that way—so I just figured I'd send my damn beer to the US. People could just as well buy them over there as in Copenhagen."

Mikkel Bjergsø and Kristian Keller brought their already popular Beer Geek Breakfast to the festival. Because they were still brewing only 50 liters of beer at a time, it had been a challenge, to say the least, to finish brewing the much larger quantities needed for this time. They didn't dare to change the approach that had triggered their success in the first place (when they eventually added coffee from a French press). Because they had to brew the stout in exactly the same way, they spent many late nights leading up to the festival; they went through a total of eighty pots of coffee before achieving their goal.

Certain logistical challenges began to present themselves in their undertaking. They were producing a hundred bottles at a time— and it took two months each time. They soon felt that it was a little ridiculous that the number wasn't greater, especially now that interest was steadily increasing. So far, they'd sold only small quantities of their homebrewed beer in the "Beer Shop," and altogether they might have brewed about 2,000 liters. After they signed the agreement with the American importer, they would be delivering beer in entirely different quantities.

Bjergsø and Keller entered an agreement with Ørbæk Brewery, located on the island of Funen. The company had just built a new, larger brewery and no longer needed their old one. The partners were welcome to borrow it. Therefore, they made frequent trips to Fyn to brew. At the time, they couldn't imagine leaving that part of the process to someone else. Also, their recipes were often significantly different from what already existed. Because no American-inspired IPAs were made in Ørbæk, they had to bring their own different ingredients. They bought most of them from homebrew shops and other breweries. For example, they got yeast from Nørrebro Bryghus and malt from Ølfabrikken, where Kristian Keller had taken a job on the side.

At Ørbæk Brewery, they could brew 2,000 liters at a time—a much higher amount than they were used to—but in practice it was just homebrewing on a larger scale.

"It was a completely crazy brewery," says Bjergsø. "It looked like something out of *The Wizard of Oz*. It was old and very difficult to brew there, so we made a lot of mistakes."

Because the brewery was a hundred years old, it created certain challenges. Among other things, it was not built to accommodate the large quantities of hops needed for their beer. Basically, they were simply scaling up their original recipes. For example, they had previously used 800 grams of hops in their 100-liter pots, but now they needed 16 kilos of hops. When it got wet, it suddenly felt like 100 kilos.

Today, all breweries in the world have what's called a whirlpool, which after boiling can start circulation. Because it uses pure centrifugal force, heavy particles collect in the middle, and all the light ones in the sides. Since at that time it was not possible to make a proper whirlpool as a homebrewer, brewers normally used "hop socks" (basically socks that you could put hops in and then tie in a knot). Subsequently, you could pull it back up again and then all the hops were gone.

Bjergsø and Keller had to use this method at the old brewery in Ørbæk—only on a much larger scale. Because they had to use a lot of hops—and because there was no whirlpool—it would get stuck in the spigots and the chiller and be almost impossible to get out again. They decided to go to a Danish fabric store, Stof 2000, where they bought large pieces of cheesecloth. Pernille Pang then sewed the pieces together on her sewing machine, so that in the end it formed a kind of giant hop sock.

At Ørbæk Brewery, they filled the sock with hops, tied a string around it, and then tossed it into the large pot.

"The first time, we put in five kilos—but we forgot that those five kilos would become outrageously heavy once they got wet. There was no extraction device, so all the evaporation wound up in the room. We couldn't see a thing while we stood there in front of this 2,000-liter boiling syrup and tried to hoist up something that suddenly weighed at least 50 kilos with the string we'd put on it. We really didn't know what we were doing—and it was dangerous as hell. That was probably the reason why Ørbæk no longer used that method and had built a new brewery."

Although Mikkeller was still relatively unknown in Denmark, interest from abroad was steadily increasing. The small microbrewery quickly began to export beer to various countries around the world. Mikkeller was no longer the hobby project it had started as—and Mikkel Bjergsø

and Kristian Keller had become dependent on each other in a way that took its toll on their relationship. In retrospect, starting Mikkeller together might not have been the best decision, because they were slowly growing apart.

The two friends disagreed about the direction they needed to take. Keller preferred to go the conventional route, brewing only the few beers they'd already had success with, while Bjergsø wanted to continue branching out. He was curious to explore what could be achieved in the world of beer.

Their different attitudes about the project didn't help. Whereas Bjergsø was unstoppable, Keller took a more casual approach. In time, the two old childhood friends realized that they should no longer be in business together. In 2007, Bjergsø offered Keller the opportunity to continue running Mikkeller; Bjergsø would then start his own new home brewery. In fact, he'd already figured out the name: Hop Burn—an American term for the kind of heartburn you get if you drink too much of the bitter hop beer that had become especially popular on the West Coast.

Mikkel Bjergsø already thought it was a cool name. When Kristian Keller decided to stop working as a brewer and, instead, pursue his dream of becoming a journalist, however, it ultimately made more sense for Mikkeller to go on. After all, it had become a relatively established name in beer circles.

Mikkeller

Mikkeller

Mikkeller's logo before and after
Kristian Keller left the company.

III

BEER REVOLUTION

With his partner gone, Mikkel Bjergsø was free to do whatever he wanted with Mikkeller—and that meant becoming even more experimental with his beers. The year after the success of Beer Geek Breakfast, he produced eight new beers, all of which were wild and challenging, for the then-current beer festival in Denmark. That prompted an immediate response. Mikkeller was crowned the year's best microbrewery by the Danish Beer Enthusiasts and, simultaneously, climbed all the way up to fifth place among the world's best microbreweries on RateBeer.

At the time, Bjergsø was still teaching full time at Det Frie Gymnasium, yet also responsible for everything in Mikkeller—from recipes to accounts to warehouse to shipping. He was busy from morning to evening, and he started to feel the pressure affecting his teaching. In defiance of his basic principles, he no longer felt he could be 100 percent prepared. Therefore, in the summer of 2008, he decided to reduce his teaching load to part-time so he could make both ends meet.

Bjergsø had ambivalent feelings, however, because he was happy in his teaching job. Det Frie Gynasium was an atypical educational institution—covered in spray paint and magic marker, filled with dilapidated furniture, and driven by an educational ideal based on students' involvement in their learning. Even more than the actual act of teaching, the school's openness really spoke to him. He'd taught elsewhere—schools where it was a struggle to teach your students—but the atypical school in Nørrebro was founded on basic democratic principles, a place where students showed up only if they wanted to.

"In general, they were dedicated students who liked me and the other teachers," he recalls. "I also really liked the overall structure, the school meetings where everything was decided and no one had more power than anyone else. The principal had the same voice as the school students. I liked that horizontal structure."

At one of the school parties, Bjergsø found common ground with two of his students. Like him, they were unimpressed with the beer they could buy at any given bar. Therefore, he persuaded the school to invest in a beer-brewing beginner set, so the three could start brewing together in the kitchen of the school cafeteria. At times, they became so preoccupied that they ended up brewing all night long before collapsing on the school couches—only waking up when they had to go straight to class.

Later, Bjergsø started a dedicated brewing committee at the school in which he educated students in brewing. He also included it as part of his curriculum when he was teaching chemistry. A few years later, two of his students, Tore Gynther and Tobias Emil Jensen, founded their own quite successful brewery, To Øl (Two Beers).

In the long run, however, it made little difference that Bjergsø had reduced his teaching hours. Approaching the Christmas holidays in 2008, he felt increasing pressure at both his teaching job and at Mikkeller. At the same time, he'd become the father of a new daughter, Stella. There simply weren't enough hours in the day. He decided to reduce his teaching hours even further, going down to two days a week, from 8 a.m. to 3:30 p.m.

By the following summer, though, he took a year off to keep up with his expanding microbrewery. In 2006, its first year as an official company, Mikkeller had total sales of a million Danish crowns (about $140,000). In 2007, that amount reached three million crowns, in 2008 nine million crowns, and in 2009 as much as fifteen million crowns. The latter was a particularly high number for a Danish microbrewery: Mikkeller had become a real business and for the first time he could draw an income.

Also, in terms of reputation, there were growing pains. In 2008, Mikkeller was once again named Brewery of the Year by the

Det Frie Gymnasium (The Free High School) in Copenhagen is renowned for being an atypical educational institution, with graffiti on the walls and an open learning environment. While Mikkel Bjergsø was employed there, he taught some of his students how to brew beer among other things.

Danish Beer Enthusiasts. In 2009—when Mikkeller had to share the award with Hornbeer—its Beer Geek Brunch Weasel climbed all the way up to number six on RateBeer's list of the best beers in the world.

However, Bjergsø still wasn't sure he wanted a future as an independent businessman in Mikkeller. He knew exactly what he found most interesting in terms of work. He loved going to tastings or festivals with Mikkeller or being able to travel, but mostly he enjoyed having colleagues, people he could play with.

"It was very difficult losing the social aspect of being a teacher. Otherwise, I would probably have done it sooner, because I was working so hard," he explains.

In the spring of 2010, the Danish trade magazine *Folkeskolen* heard about the schoolteacher who had started brewing beer and interviewed him under the headline: "The Teacher- Brewer." At the end of the interview, he was asked which of the two worlds he would choose if he were given an ultimatum.

"If I was told that I could only do one of these things for the rest of my life, I don't think I would choose Mikkeller. Then I would choose the school," he replied at the time.

They were two vastly different professional lives. One happened at the school, where he showed up in the morning to teach twenty-two students in his class. When the day ended, he'd hang out with the other teachers in the evening, drinking beers and eating together. His second profession took place alone at a brewery or on the ground floor of his apartment, where he sat at his computer doing administrative work.

"At Mikkeller, I sat alone, working, or I packed pallets by myself in a garage in Valby. I was used to having a very social work life—and I really liked being a teacher much better. I loved being at Det Frie Gymnasium with all my colleagues and students. I'd never dreamed of having to be self-employed. I don't come from a family where people do that kind of thing.

Also, there are risks with that. I didn't make beer to become independent—I did it because I believed I could make something that was more interesting than what was on the market," he comments.

Mikkeller had become a recognizable name internationally—and an increasing number of prominent visitors arrived from abroad. Bjergsø didn't have his own brewery, however, so he had no actual locale where he could bring them. He thought they'd find it strange to be sitting on the ground floor of his apartment, where he had his desk. Also, he didn't exactly enjoy taking his guests to either smoky bodegas or one of those typical Irish bars filled with old men with huge bellies, mugs, and loud rock music blaring from the speakers.

"In my eyes, there was always something wrong at those bars," he says. "There was always something that wasn't as it should be. What I was looking for was a place where everything worked together, so you could have a holistic experience—at the very least where nothing removed focus or disturbed experiencing the beer. At most bars, beer ads are hanging all over the walls, but I don't think it makes sense to be sitting there drinking Hoegaarden while you're staring at a Guinness sign. In my eyes, the environment needed to be fairly neutral. Therefore, the idea arose to try to create a place that represented Mikkeller—where the beer was the main focus."

Bjergsø decided to open his own bar, one that would be like no other. Back then, most bars looked the same, no matter where in the

Mikkeller's first bar on Viktoriagade, in the Vesterbro neighborhood of Copenhagen.

Mikkel Bjergsø collaborated with design studio Femmes Régionales to develop Mikkeller's first bar. He wanted a bar with a lighter and more Scandinavian aesthetic than those that existed at the time.

world you were: dark, male-dominated places that in his perspective weren't very inviting—and not at all geared toward women. Instead, he wanted a bar that was brighter and more Nordic, a place where they not only made good beer but also had an eye for detail.

"At that time, there were almost no modern beer bars in the world," observes Bjergsø. "Almost all of them were pubs—and I have nothing against pubs—but I thought it was a shame that almost all of them were man caves. When I go out, I also want to be with people other than hardcore beer nerds. That's why I wanted to make a beer bar that appealed to different types of people."

Naturally, the bar had to also have his own beer on tap, so he could invite his guests to visit—a kind of microbrewery showroom.

"I care about details. It's important to me that there's a sense of wholeness to things. You might be sitting with the world's best beer in your hand, but if there's shitty music coming out of the speakers, ugly art on the walls, or the bartender is rude, it's hard to have a positive experience. It all needs to be interconnected—and that just wasn't happening in the bar scene at the time."

To develop the bar, Bjergsø collaborated with Femmes Régionales, a women-operated Danish design studio. They designed typical fashion shows for brands—but he happened to know the boss, Caroline Hansen, through his half-brother. Since they represented something completely different from the established bar scene, he asked them to submit three different bids for a concept that was brighter—one with Nordic aesthetics. He chose what spoke directly to his idea of good taste, and from here they jointly rethought everything known about traditional bars. For example, they decided that people should be able to order beer in small glasses with a stem, something entirely different from the typical pints that one got at most bars.

"It was a totally new concept at that time. But if you're a twenty-year-old woman who doesn't go in much for craft beer—maybe you think it tastes strange—then it's a lot to drink all at once. This way, you could taste smaller samples," he says.

On the other hand, that the bar was located on Viktoriagade in Copenhagen's Vesterbro neighborhood was purely coincidental. Originally, Bjergsø had found another locale on historic Istedgade, where the bar Simpelt V is today. The iconic street had become a main destination in this part of town, so opening a bar there seemed obvious; but after a bad experience with the seller—and another opportunity suddenly surfaced on Viktoriagade—he decided to choose the atypical solution. Although there were no more than 500 meters between the two streets, there was a world of difference.

"I was actually a little scared of being on Istedgade," admits Bjergsø, "because I wanted to serve wild beer from the world's best breweries. I honestly didn't mind that most people only wanted a big draft beer. I didn't really want those customers anyway, because then my employees would have to explain themselves all the time—and people still wouldn't understand any of it. Instead, I ended up on Viktoriagade, a completely fucked-up part of the city that no one came to at the time. The area was always in the news because of crime—drug dealing, prostitution, stabbings—so I knew no one would ever be there unless they wanted to go to my bar."

The locale spoke well to the philosophy that Bjergsø had already begun formulating about not spending money on marketing. He didn't want people to buy his beer just because they'd had some advertisement shoved down their throats. If so, the likelihood of their being disappointed would be greater. Since so many people were accustomed to drinking Carlsberg, they just didn't have the right frame of mind for trying something new.

"On the other hand, if they bought a beer because their friend had told them to try

At the opening of Mikkeller's first bar on Viktoriagade, in Vesterbro (May 5, 2010). At top, Mikkeller's first employee, Thomas Schøn, giving a short speech while standing on a beer crate.

Mikkeller, the likelihood of their having a good experience was also greater," he says. "The same with the bar. The experience is different if you make an effort to get there, instead of just walking down the street and have a quick one at some random place. Since then, I've deliberately put my bars in places where people had to make an effort to get there. Maybe that wasn't the best business decision, but at least people came because they decided to come. And then they always came again, because we had the world's best beer on tap."

It was a sensation in the summer of 2010 when the bar on Viktoriagade opened with twenty alternating beers on tap. In addition to Mikkeller's own beers, you could get beers from 3 Floyds Brewing and AleSmith, voted the best and second-best breweries in the world, respectively. A couple of years before, Mikkel Bjergsø had contacted the two well-known

Label from the beer Vesterbro Pilsner—a tribute to Viktoriagade, where Mikkeller's first bar opened. The street is known for a large heart sculpture, erected in 1989, that over the years has been painted with countless different messages. In 2018, Mikkeller's art director, Keith Shore, decorated it.

microbreweries, which he regarded as some of his idols within the industry, to see if he could visit them. He hadn't expected anything to come from his inquiries, which was the reason why he wrote to both—because he figured that the chance would be twice as great.

"I never expected them to say yes, because what good would it do them for me to come over there?" he says. "Nobody collaborated on brewing back then, so why should they let me in and show me how they did things?"

To his surprise, he was invited inside both American microbreweries. That led to a friendship—and now, in addition to Mikkeller's own brand, you could also get their beers in the new bar on Viktoriagade. It attracted attention, not only in Denmark, but also abroad.

"There were only a couple of bars in Copenhagen that carried exciting beers, which usually meant they might have been to Belgium to pick up something. Mikkeller had been named the world's third best out of many thousands of breweries in the world—we also had the world's best and second-best brewery on tap. In the US, 3 Floyds was almost impossible to get hold of because it was so ridiculously hyped. Now you could get it at Vesterbro in Copenhagen, so there were people who flew here just for that."

Mikkeller was already being sold in over twenty different countries, and now Bjergsø even had his own bar. Reluctantly, he quit his teaching job to go all-in on conquering the globe with his microbrewery.

"It was really hard to quit, but I had employees at Mikkeller depending on me to pay their salary," he explains. "At the same time, I could see that everything was about to really take off. It was totally crazy when I opened the bar. Two thousand people showed up—and the Danish TV-news covered it live, proclaiming it 'beer's answer to Noma,' which had just been named the world's best restaurant. It took off in a way I never anticipated. People flew in from all over the world, Americans, Australians, Japanese, just to drink beer at the bar on Viktoriagade. I was curious to see where it was all going."

Although this new chapter in Mikkel Bjergsø's life had started with a bang, there was still some way to go before Mikkeller's path to world domination. As part of its atypical concept, the bar on Viktoriagade would also be open on Sundays. At that time in Denmark, almost every business closed on Sundays, so there was almost no place where you could drink a beer. Bjergsø wanted to be able to drink beer on Sundays, however. That was his decision—although it took some time before locals got used to it.

"On one of the first Sundays, we made only 250 crowns. Totally ridiculous. People just weren't used to beer bars in that way—but they would be."

IV

NOMADIC BREWER

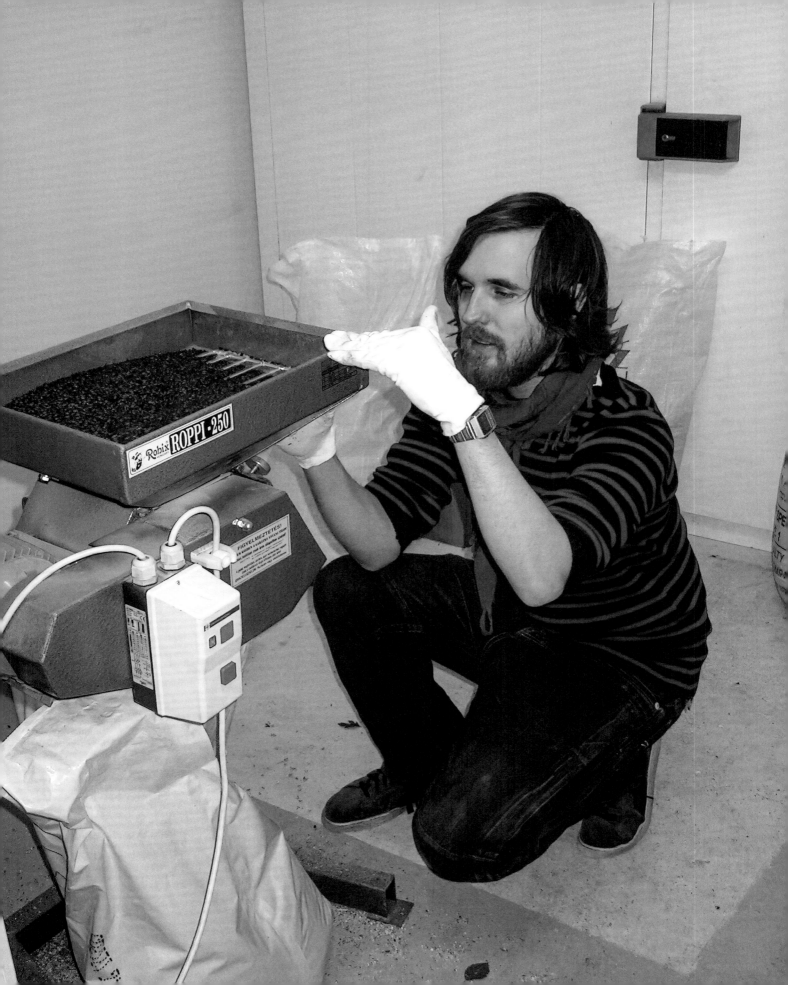

When Mikkel Bjergsø was featured in *Beer-Advocate* in 2010, under the headline "The Godfather of Gypsy Brewing," it not only heralded the beginning of a new era—it was also the first time the term "gypsy brewer" had appeared (at least for such a wide audience). The term described a way of being a brewer in which you didn't own your own brewery premises; instead, you either rented from other breweries to use their boilers or you decided to make them responsible for the actual production.

Bjergsø wasn't really interested in running his own brewery. This way, he could keep his fixed costs low and, instead, cultivate the freedom to think both creatively and big. Although it was impressive at that time for a microbrewery to produce twenty different beers in one year, he had the potential to make over a hundred different beers—and he soon did. He was upsetting the traditional model, yet he viewed it as a natural development, a democratization of the brewing scene. After all, not everyone can simply walk into a bank, get a loan, and build their own brewery. By becoming a nomadic brewer, you could free yourself from having to earn enough money to keep your own brewery running. Bjergsø saw similarities to other industries in which it was customary not to own your own means of production. For example, in the fashion industry, designers were responsible for creative development yet produced their clothes elsewhere in the world.

After some time, Mikkel Bjergsø had to admit that he didn't really find the practical side of the brewing process particularly interesting. It began to feel like the same thing over and over again. It was too mechanical, like standing in a factory all day and pushing the same buttons. He was far more concerned with the creative aspect: coming up with ideas, creating new recipes, and exploring which nooks and crannies one could reach into. This way, he could leave the rest to the experts.

"There were some Americans who did the same thing, but it was all hush-hush. Nobody wanted to admit it—but I did, because I thought there were a lot of benefits to doing it that way. Instead of paying back bank loans, I could concentrate on inventing new recipes," he says.

Not everyone viewed it that way, though. Although microbrewing was, in a way, an industry in rapid development, in other ways it was quite conservative, conforming to a history dating back several hundred years. You had to be careful not to challenge norms too much. Once he had become known as the industry's leading nomadic brewer, Bjergsø could sense it. He often had to listen to people who thought he couldn't call Mikkeller a brewery when he didn't even own his own physical brewery.

At a tasting at The Bishops Arms in Stockholm, some Swedish brewers bought a ticket solely to ask hyper-critical questions. Both the brewers and Bjergsø were a little drunk, so it ended with all of them sitting around shouting at each other. Another bar in Stockholm, Akkurat, which was named the world's best beer bar for several years, even refused to serve beer from nomadic breweries. In Denmark, Munkebo Brewery, in particular, was on the warpath: the master brewer there suggested introducing a sticker that read "BBB" and could be put on beer sold in stores. The BBB was supposed to stand for "Brewed at the Brewery by the Brewer," so that those who cared about those things could run rings around breweries like Mikkeller.

When Bjergsø won the most prestigious award at the official Danish Beer Festival in 2013—Danish Beer Enthusiasts had determined that he "has really managed to go a step further from hand brewing to a significant player in the beer market"—it prompted even further criticism. Several brewers on the Danish scene had a hard time understanding how someone could be named "Microbrewery of the Year" when they didn't even own a brewery. And could you even call yourself a brewer if you didn't own your own facilities? After the selection, a group of brewers who had sat together during the selection and wanted to express their dissatisfaction called him.

"They were angry that I was able to win, when I didn't even own my own brewery. So, I had to explain to them that I didn't give myself the fucking prize—and anyway, I really couldn't give a damn."

In 2007, Mikkel Bjergsø needed to find a new brewery that could brew his beer. He'd been using the Gourmet Brewery in Roskilde for a while, and one day they offered to buy Mikkeller and take over the brand. Bjergsø wasn't interested, however, so he told them that they could forget it. Shortly afterwards, they informed him that they no longer had enough space to brew his beer. He was looking to move on to greener pastures when Beer Factory, his distributor at that time in Denmark, suggested that he contact a brewer in northern Belgium who specialized in brewing for others—an ideal collaboration (at least on paper) for a nomadic brewer. He approached the Belgian company De Proefbrouwerij, and shortly thereafter its master brewer, Dirk Naudts, a bald man with a mild facial expression, was making both a Belgian ale called Monk's Elixir and a lager named Draft Bear for Mikkeller. Before long, a West Coast IPA called Green Gold and Mikkeller's first Christmas beer, Santa's Little Helper, followed—and the new partnership was off and running.

At least that's how Mikkel Bjergsø saw it—but Dirk Naudts hesitated. The Belgian master brewer was accustomed to brewing only a few recipes in large quantities; now, he was dealing with a customer who was spitting out recipes at an alarming rate. After the first four beers, Naudts suggested brewing only them, to which the Dane replied: "Um, I also have just a few other ideas…."

In 2008, when Bjergsø expressed his desire to make barrel-aged beer, Naudts rejected the idea on the spot. It just couldn't be done—not in a country as traditional as Belgium. To be a bit accommodating, however, he suggested putting wood chips in the beer. Bjergsø wanted no part in that. The whole point of the experiment was to utilize oxidation from the barrels. He wanted the beers barrel-aged. After a bit of a tug of war, he won through sheer stubbornness, and today the De Proef Brewery has an entire building filled with only Mikkeller barrels.

"His first response was usually no whenever I came up with a new recipe," says Bjergsø, "but he'd always wind up accepting the challenge. It was funny, because Dirk actually liked producing different kinds of beer and being challenged. He just wasn't used to it, so it took a little persuasion."

Once Dirk Naudts became accustomed to the idea, he also realized that experimenting and developing beer with a man like Bjergsø could be both fruitful and exciting. A little over ten years earlier, in 1996, the Belgian master brewer had founded the Flemish brewery with his wife, Saskia Waerniers, who, like her husband, was trained in biochemistry and had specialized in brewing. Although for years they brewed their own beer under the name Reinaert, they established themselves primarily as a so-called rental brewery making beer for nomadic breweries. In fact, their original intention was to create their own brewery so they could produce beer based on recipes from various creative beer people.

Dirk Naudts' primary interest was the scientific part of beer brewing. He was a man who made sure to invest every time there were technological breakthroughs, to be at the forefront of every requirement he had to meet from his clients. When he and Mikkel Bjergsø first became acquainted in 2007, he was fully engaged in building an impressive research and development department. For the Belgian master brewer who had recently celebrated the tenth anniversary of his

brewery, meeting the insistent but creative Danish beer inventor turned out to be a welcome challenge. Bjergsø was a totally different experience. Whereas Naudts' other customers wouldn't normally reveal the fact that they brewed beer at the De Proef Brewery, the Dane stood a hundred percent behind being a nomadic brewer. He had no interest in having his own brewery—he was interested in finding the perfect person to turn his recipes into the world's best beer. Naudts fully understood that approach.

"We're ridiculously different," admits Bjergsø, "but we complement each other really well. Dirk doesn't like all the commercial stuff—he wants to dive into the technical aspects of beer brewing. And I don't like to brew beer, buy equipment, and repair pumps—I just want to come up with recipes

Belgian brewmaster Dirk Naudts from De Proef Brewery, which has brewed the majority of Mikkeller's beer for many years.

and challenge beer styles, marketing, and expression. It makes for a good combination. I don't think it would have worked if we each had different ambitions. However, Dirk wants to be the best in the world in his field, and I want to be the best in the world in mine. So we fit really well together."

After a few years of collaborating, Mikkeller and the De Proef Brewery threw themselves into their first major project together. Bjergsø had the idea for a Single Hop series of beers, and Naudts and his team would be the ones to deliver it. At that time, the type of hops that had been used never appeared on the labels of any beer bottles. Therefore, it was impossible for people to understand why one IPA, for example, had more of a citrusy flavor, while the next one tasted more floral.

Bjergsø was determined to change all that—not only to educate consumers about beer, but also so he could understand it himself. When he drank IPAs from the US, they tasted different from those from Europe, which could only be due to the use of different hops.

"I think it's my background as a schoolteacher," he comments. "I like to learn more about what I'm spending my time on, and I like to teach others as well if I'm passionate about something. It's nice to be able to share something cool you've discovered with others. It had become important for me to know what I drank and why it tasted the way it did—and I wanted to expose others to that."

Working with the De Proef Brewery, Bjergsø set out to make a series of beers, all of them brewed using the same recipe with one deviation: different hops in each beer. Ann Van Holle, a PhD student from the University of Ghent, was hired to lead the project. Initially, she and the staff at the Belgian brewery analyzed various types of hops from around the world. Among other challenges they faced, they had to deal with the fact that there was no guarantee that the hops they ordered were the hops they received. Therefore, Mikkeller and the De Proef Brewery decided to procure hops directly from different hop farmers.

At that time, IPAs consisted of a mixture of different hops, but Mikkel Bjergsø wanted to learn on his own how Simcoe, for example, tasted. That hop, he discovered, had a strong taste of pineapple or melon. In this way he familiarized himself with different types of hops and became much more knowledgeable about them. Ultimately, it became a series of different single-hop beers aimed at teaching consumers that hops are not simply a taste, but also an ingredient with numerous flavors and nuances. In the wake of the launch, consumers everywhere began to make other demands.

The different types of hops were rated on RateBeer, making it attractive for breweries to use the highest rated to lure customers into their store. Ultimately, the series led to hops being much more clearly marked on the list of ingredients, as they are today. Even today, the Single Hop series is one of the projects Bjergsø is most proud of, specifically because it helped educate both beer drinkers and brewers all over the world.

"Back then, I thought it was a shame that knowledge about beer was so backward compared to wine. I wanted to raise people's understanding of beer to another level. All of a sudden, consumers were learning that not all hops were the same—that some tasted like grass, some like melon, some like peppermint. People were discovering that hops provided outrageously different flavor nuances on the palette. I would venture to say that *that* series has been completely revolutionary worldwide."

Since Bjergsø founded Mikkeller, the company has distributed over two thousand beers. Many of them have, in one way or another, managed to attract attention—either because of experimental inventions, strange ingredients, striking labels, or crazy names.

Together with De Proef Brewery, Mikkeller issued the Single Hop series, consisting of 21 IPAs brewed with different hops, for example Cascade, Amarillo, and Centennial.

In 2010, Mikkeller released two beers called Oatgoop and Wheatgoop, which were the result of a fusion brew with the American brewery 3 Floyds Brewing. More than the names, the colorful labels on these beers attracted attention. In addition to a laughing skull with green, ferocious eyes on the brown bottles, the number 69 appeared, a reference to the infamous Youth House on Jagtvej 69 in Copenhagen (it had been demolished three years earlier). Many of the students whom he was still teaching at the time at Det Frie Gymnasium were extremely dismayed by the demolition; therefore, Bjergsø expressed his sympathy in his own way.

Mikkeller's ever-growing catalog also includes beers such as Illuminaughty, Salmon Pants, and Beer Geek Brunch Weasel. The latter is made with coffee beans that have taken a ride, so to speak, through a Vietnamese weasel, the luwak, which roams around Southeast Asian coffee plantations. Another time, Mikkeller bought truffles for 45,000 crowns (about $6,100) for the beer Forager. For the launch of the Swedish band Bob Hund's latest album, Mikkeller made, at their request, an IPA on licorice pipes called Dance After My Licorice IPA.

For Mikkel Bjergsø, however, it has never been about pushing the envelope just for the sake of doing so. On the other hand, he has always been determined to test the boundaries of what beer can be, as when Mikkeller created the beer 1000 IBU, an attempt to make the most hopped beer in the world. At other times, mistakes have led to successes: he once made a typing mistake in a recipe, and a Norwegian brewery ending up adding one hundred times more vanilla sugar than intended to a batch of Imperial Stout. At first, both he and the brewery were convinced that the 10,000 bottles were ruined, but the contents yet again turned out not to be so absurd. The new beers were dubbed Beer Geek Vanilla Shake—and ended up becoming Mikkeller's best-selling beer in 2013.

Top left: label for the beer Oatgoop, which Mikkeller brewed together with the American brewery 3 Floyds. The number 69 is a reference to the former Youth Center on Jagtvej in Copenhagen.

Top right: the launch of a new album from the Swedish band Bob Hund, for which Mikkeller made an IPA with licorice pipes in it.

Bottom: a label for the beer 1000 IBU.

Even after Mikkel Bjergsø went from being a homebrewer to a nomadic one, he kept his small 100-liter homebrewing plant for a long time. Occasionally, he'd brew new batches of Mikkeller's X Imperial Stout there. For years, the beer stayed in the top 50 of the best in the world on RateBeer. Thus, Bjergsø insisted on making it in exactly the same old-fashioned way: without temperature control and without any pH adjustment to the water.

Also, for purely nostalgic reasons, he enjoyed being a nomadic brewer who could benefit from the respective strength of different breweries. He has collaborated with breweries in England, Scotland, and the US—but also in Norway, more specifically the brewery Nøgne Ø and later Lervig, where the water is particularly suited to dark types of beer. And when ideas for new beer have spontaneously fermented on his drawing board, he often turns his attention to Belgian brewers, who are extremely good at brewing that type of beer because they have a long history of doing so.

More than anyone else, Bjergsø has collaborated for years with Dirk Naudts, whom he considers the best in the world. He completely trusts the Belgian master brewer to execute his ideas. Still, Bjergsø has never delegated inventing recipes. He considers that his strength, and he has never been comfortable letting others in on it.

Since Mikkeller's breakthrough in beer circles, Bjergsø has received beers regularly from all over the world. Especially during his first few years, he tasted many different beers. The raw materials often gave him new ideas either to try something similar or to make a change in something he'd already been fiddling around with. Still, he's taken inspiration from far more than just other brewers; he's also been able to build on chefs, winemakers, or coffee baristas who take a different approach to tastes and aromas.

Even after Mikkeller grew, for many years they resisted establishing fixed production plans. New beers have come when they've come—which is frequently. In Mikkel Bjergsø's own view, he's not really imaginative by nature. On the other hand, he is curious, and that's an advantage. When he encounters new ingredients that he hasn't tasted before, he instinctively becomes curious about how he can use them. In fact, his ruminating about most recipes begins that way. He might be drinking an Altbier in Düsseldorf and feel like trying to produce something similar himself, or he might be eating a cake and think it would be interesting to either make a beer that tastes like it or one that can complement it.

To this day, Mikkel Bjergsø travels as often as he can to Belgium to see how his upcoming beers are doing. Today, the small, unassuming town of Lochristi, on the outskirts of Ghent in East Flanders, is home to one of the most advanced high-tech breweries in the world. Before entering, you have to rinse the soles of your shoes in distilled water. It's like opening the door to a kind of beer university, where professors and PhD students walk around in white coats and blue work uniforms, carefully monitoring the large steel brewing vessels. The associated R&D lab is equipped with instruments such as a humidity meter and devices for distilling fusel alcohol, gas chromatography, and mass spectrometry—along with a "secret department" where laboratory technicians research hops, malt, spices, and yeast. Among other things, they can analyze aromas in hops all the way down to the molecular level, and they maintain a yeast bank with 20,000 different yeast strings, all of which they have mapped and stored.

When they began their collaboration, Mikkel Bjergsø was the only employee at Mikkeller—in fact, he wasn't even a full-time employee at the time. De Proef, on the other hand, had ten employees and brewed 10,000 hectoliters of beer a year. Today, they brew about 100,000 hectoliters and have over fifty employees. They are currently building five new brewhouses, designed by Dirk Naudts, and have hired two full-time welders to build over the next four years. By then, they will be able to brew eight different beers at once— and more than sixty different beers a day.

As Bjergsø has described it, the De Proef Brewery is pure "Willy Wonka Beer Factory." He's been able to turn to them whenever he has devised a recipe for a new beer with ingredients as quirky as Chinese mint leaves, unwashed seaweed from Iceland's western fjords, yuzu from Japan, or avocado leaves from Mexico. From there, the Belgian master brewer has taken care of the practical end and turned the recipe into something that can be drunk with pleasure.

Almost fifteen years have passed since Bjergsø began his collaboration with Belgian master brewer Dirk Naudts; since then, few people have been as fundamental to Mikkeller's success. Their partnership has resulted in countless beers and wild projects. After the Single Hop series, they crafted a similar one, but with different types of yeast. They've also produced a series of barrel-aged, spontaneously fermented beers under the general name of the Mikkeller Spontan Series. Dirk Naudts and the employees at De Proef Brewery have even duplicated the water from Lake Michigan, which is particularly neutral and thus good for brewing. Naudts and Bjergsø have also developed a large number of non-alcoholic beers together; the development of a new yeast strain has made it possible to brew non-alcoholic beers with stronger taste.

To this day, Mikkel Bjergsø trusts that no matter what unpredictable ingredients appear on his list, the beer experts in Lochristi can solve it. Once he comes up with a recipe, he writes down a detailed guide in which he states, for example, the amount of malt in grams. Dirk Naudts and his people then do the testing and ultimately brew the beer that comes in the bottle. For both partners, it has been a perfect collaboration—or, as the master brewer once described it, "a long marriage that has gradually found solid and stable ground."

"People couldn't taste a damn thing. A lot of mistakes were being made in the business—but because it was microbrewery, many people thought it should taste like that."

– Mikkel Bjergsø

Dirk Naudts and Mikkel Bjergsø. The vast majority of Mikkeller's beer is brewed at the De Proef Brewery in Lochristi, on the outskirts of Ghent in Belgium.

In time, criticism from the more conservative brewers began to die down. By 2014, there were an estimated forty nomadic brewers in Denmark. Only a few years earlier, Bjergsø had been the first and only one. Today it's a long-accepted approach to brewing.

"I was successful at it and then others were successful at it—and that allowed even more people to do it. And then it wasn't interesting to talk more about it anymore," he observes.

At the same time, the industry has made incredible advances. Although the cultural history of beer dates back more than 8,000 years, developments over the last forty years have been pronounced. After then-US President Jimmy Carter lifted the ban on homebrewing in 1979, a kind of revolution in beer started on the American continent: homebrewers and microbreweries began to push the boundaries of how beer could taste. Anchor and Sierra Nevada were some of the first and most prominent craft breweries in the 1980s.

The microbrewery scene slowly matured throughout the 1990s and further into the 2000s, when it really began to gain momentum. That also happened in Denmark, which went, in just a few years, from nothing to being one of the leading microbrewery countries in the world. Of course, Belgium, Germany, England, and the Czech Republic had a far more developed and established beer culture—but theirs were founded on ancient and traditional breweries that had been making the same beers for many hundreds of years. Denmark was at the forefront of the new scene. New Danish microbreweries were particularly motivated by a showdown with consumer beer, especially Carlsberg, who with a few exceptions such as Hancock, Thisted, and Refsvindinge, completely dominated the market. Danish Beer Enthusiasts also led the effort to create more diversity—as in Belgium, for example. In time, new breweries introduced new types of beer such as wheat beer, porter, or maybe even pale ales.

Before long, however, Carlsberg made the same move. There was still a long way to go before seeing the IPAs that had begun to appear on the US West Coast. India Pale Ales actually originated in England, but American brewers developed that genre of beer into the more extreme types starting to emerge around the turn of the millennium.

When Mikkeller began crafting IPAs, virtually no one in Denmark knew or was interested in that type of beer. Ølfabrikken tried their hand at it, and Brøckhouse was producing a single IPA, but it had a more subdued character, one more in line with English traditions. From 2005 on, people began to take the new American traditions seriously on the Danish beer scene. After that, beer got wilder and wilder: it became increasingly trendy, for example, to increase the IBU (International Bitterness Units) in IPAs. First it had to be at 100, then 200—and then Mikkeller made one at 1,000. Also, for the first time, other types of beer, such as imperial stouts, found their way into the market. Mikkeller made a version called Black, the sole purpose of which was to make the beer as strong as possible.

New microbreweries started springing up everywhere; it was all about pushing the boundaries of beer-making. Therefore, it wasn't surprising that the next big trend was pastry stouts, which were sweet, dark beers crammed full of all sorts of ingredients not previously associated with the beer industry. It might be beer that tasted like cake. On a more general level, however, people were not particularly adroit at tasting different types of beer.

"People couldn't taste a damn thing," says Bjergsø. "A lot of mistakes were being made in the business—but because it was microbrewery, many people thought it should taste like that. Suddenly it was sour, and then people thought it should be sour. It was similar to a few years earlier when natural wine became popular in Denmark. At first, it tasted awful, because it was made completely wrong, except that no one knew it. Even if you talked to a sommelier, he'd say that the lumps were actually due to fermentation, or something like that."

In the late 2000s, one microbrewery in Denmark became a kind of darling of the industry, simply because they grew all their own ingredients—even though their beer in Mikkel Bjergsø's eyes tasted terrible. He was convinced that it was poorly produced. So, he bought fifteen of their beers and then sent them down to the laboratory at the De Proef Brewery in Belgium.

"It turned out that some of the beers were totally unsuitable for drinking, because they were so infected that it was almost harmful to your health. At the same time, sommeliers at Michelin-star restaurants were serving them and talking them up—even though they tasted ridiculously awful."

After 2010, the microbrewery scene really took off. Even though these special beers weren't found in everyone's home, they were no longer only for the specially initiated. Microbreweries started to open their own bars, including Mikkeller's first bar in Copenhagen's Vesterbro area. Within the industry, barrel-aged beer became a huge craze, and some people even started buying vintage beers and building beer cellars at home.

In time, fruity sour beer was in—as much fruit as possible had to be stuffed into the beer. Five or six years ago, Hazy IPAs took over for a while. Earlier, there had been talk of "chill haze" in the industry. If you put a beer in the fridge and it became cloudy while in there, it was "chill haze"—that is, a mistake in the beer. In the mid-2010s, however, beer suddenly had to be as hazy and rich as possible. The iconic Vermont-based brewery The Alchemist kicked off that trend with its beer Heady Topper, which quickly became hugely popular. Eventually, the company had to build an entire brewery to produce that specific beer, just so they could keep up with demand.

The last few years have seen increased demand for non-alcoholic beer. Across the globe, people have started drinking less alcohol. This trend also applies to young people: it's no longer about how much you can drink, but instead about deciding what you drink. The trend is especially challenging for big breweries, and many of them are currently suffering as a direct consequence of it. In the US, microbreweries now occupy about forty percent of the market, whereas Budweiser's market share, for example, has fallen significantly in the last twenty years. On the whole, competition is greater than ever before. Where microbreweries previously had to fight with the big guns for shelf space, now they really have to fight with each other.

Recently, the industry has seen a return to more traditional beers. Instead of cramming a lot of different ingredients into one beer, focus has turned to craftsmanship. In fact, it's usually more difficult to make a good pale ale at three percent than a jet-black and viscous imperial stout—it's much harder to hide the flaws in the former. For three years in a row, Bjergsø has proclaimed the coming year to be "the year of the lager." A number of factors indicate that it's finally happening. The American brewery 3 Sons Brewing, among the most hyped every year at the Mikkeller Beer Celebration, has noticed that people now come into its tap room in Florida to drink lagers. Pastry stouts and hazy IPAs have seen their day.

"A few years ago, people wrote to ask what the hell I was talking about, because no one was drinking 'craft' pilsners at the time," he explains. "But almost all the 'collabs' we're making at the moment are actually lagers, or some type of lager. That's what brewers drink, too. They drink lagers and serve IPAs to their customers. It's interesting, because customers dictate trends, but sometimes *you* have to change them—or else nothing happens. Because there are enough damn IPAs in the world."

In the last few years, Bjergsø has turned his attention toward more traditional types of beer instead of, for example, wild IPAs. However, he says that first he needed to expand the spectrum of what beer can actually be—how it can taste—and thus educate people in proper beer tasting. That approach has given him much greater latitude to return to what is simple and focus on good craftsmanship.

"When I made my first IPA, people thought it was really extreme, that it was undrinkable, because there was so much hops in it," comments Bjergsø. "Today, people can barely get enough hops in their beer. It's cool that it's gone that way—that people have actually become receptive to extreme and wild things. You're better at tasting whether a lager is any good if you know about beer on a deeper level. If all you've ever drunk is Carlsberg, you can't evaluate anything. It's like with food, you need a universe to compare it to."

For Bjergsø, in a way, it involves taking the beer world back, and he senses that something is afoot. Only a few years ago, he experienced how much the members of Mikkeller's beer club, who receive a packet of eight new beers a month, grumbled like crazy if there was even one lager among them. Today they'll gladly accept three—enthusiastically.

"In my eyes, the beer world has gotten out of hand. There's so much hazy IPA and crap like that, stuff that tastes awful and that brewing-wise is pure shit. It has become too crazy—I'd rather try to make some insanely good beers, just as people have been brewing them for ages. There are places in Bamberg, Germany with nineteenth-generation brewers. In theory, they've been brewing the same beer for 600 years. That's cool, and I'd like to focus on that, because beer is a craft that an insane number of good people have refined for centuries. It's not just about stuffing marshmallows in a beer and serving it."

In the last few years, Mikkel Bjergsø has focused on returning to more traditional beers. Within that process, Mikkeller has worked with two classic breweries, Gaffel and Uerige, located in Cologne and Düsseldorf in Germany.

V

MIKKELLER & FRIENDS

One day in 2008, Mikkel Bjergsø was holding a beer tasting at a kiosk on Vesterbro in Copenhagen, and one of the employees came up to him afterwards. He was studying rhetoric at college and was writing an essay about Mikkeller. Therefore, he wanted to greet the founder and introduce himself. Finally, he said: "Besides, I'm going to redo your website, because right now it looks like shit."

Bjergsø had initially gotten one of his friends to make his website. He wasn't especially skilled at that kind of thing, which became clear when he subsequently had to make changes—like updating information on new beers—and it took him a thousand years to enter the right HTML codes.

"I was sitting there lost in a jungle of codes, trying to figure it out. If I wrote *here,* would it come up on the screen *there?* I had no idea what I was doing, so the website was a mess that had never really been updated," he says.

However, Thomas Schøn, his new rhetoric student acquaintance, had experience in programming, so he was given free rein to remake it. Before long, he became Mikkeller's first employee, given the diverse task of helping with everything. He became an integral part of the microbrewery: every time Mikkel Bjergsø packed beer in the warehouse, stacked it in the back of his Mercedes Vito, and delivered it for tastings in Copenhagen, Schøn was there.

When the bar in Vesterbro was about to open in May of 2010, Bjergsø needed a bar manager. He already knew Jannik Sahlholdt, the former bar manager at Ølbaren, the first real beer bar in Copenhagen. Sahlholdt became Mikkeller's second full-time employee (after Schøn).

During the first few years, the staff at Mikkeller consisted mostly of friends and barflies. The carpenter Nikolaj Eis, who had previously worked with the design studio Femmes Régionales, was hired to build the first bar. He decided to stay and eventually became a full-time employee; since then, he has built the vast majority of Mikkeller's bars and restaurants. Bjergsø's former student Tore Gynther was initially hired as a bartender, later took a job at the warehouse, and eventually ended up in one of the first administrative positions at the company's former office on Vesterbrogade.

Another former student, Frank Hilmer Borring Petersen, started working in Mikkeller as a busboy when he was only seventeen years old. When Mikkel Bjergsø taught him, he found him a little annoying. So, Bjergsø told the bar manager that he couldn't recommend him—and that he shouldn't refrain from throwing him out again if he couldn't behave properly. Today, Petersen is E-Commerce Manager in Mikkeller, and he and Mikkel are still friends.

Anyone who knew either Mikkel Bjergsø or someone who knew him could easily procure a job with the company—and from there, it wasn't far to reach the top, which happened for a number of people. No one ever looked at anybody's résumé.

"I couldn't care less about someone's education," admits Bjergsø. "If you only learn about the world from what you read in books, you have no idea what it really looks like. I'm sure you can learn things, but you also learn a lot of constraints. I hear that whenever I talk to people who have gone to Copenhagen Business School. They learn how not to. I've done it completely differently, because I'm not trained. For me, it's more about personality."

Then there was the magician Rasmus "Magic" Malmstrøm, the boyfriend of Pernille Pang's best friend (which is how Mikkel Bjergsø got to know him). Malmstrøm—a former photographer and a guitarist for the pop singer Aura—became interested in magic and taught himself all sorts of tricks by nerding out on YouTube videos. Therefore, he was invited whenever Mikkeller opened new bars or held events. Malmstrøm would run around doing magic tricks and holding events for those

present. It was a win-win. He could practice and acquire a lot of new clients, and Mikkeller had its very own staff magician.

Pernille Pang also worked for Mikkeller—even though both Bjergsø and she had tried for years to keep her out of the business. They didn't want to mix their private and professional lives. While writing her thesis in Media and Communication Studies at Roskilde University, she was employed at *Politiken*'s then-free newspaper *24 Hours*. At that time, a fierce competition among a number of new free newspapers was unfolding, so those publications were headhunting many newly hatched journalists. After she'd been there for three years, the newspaper was acquired by *metroXpress*; at about the same time she was going on maternity leave with their first

Mikkel Bjergsø and Tore Gynther during Mikkeller Beer Celebration Copenhagen. The two got to know each other when they were teacher and student, respectively, at Det Frie Gymnasium, and Mikkel taught the students how to brew. Tore worked for a few years in various positions at Mikkeller, but today he owns his own successful beer brand, To Øl.

child, Stella. Instead, she stopped to freelance, which she had been doing for some years, when she was contacted by the Danish publisher Gyldendal, who wanted to write a book about Mikkeller.

Afterwards, Pang moved into Mikkeller's head office, located at that time on Vesterbrogade, where she learned everything there was to know about the company. A whole new world opened before her, one she previously regarded as rather dull. She was forced to familiarize herself with everything, to learn all the different types of beer, for example. When *Mikkeller's Book of Beer* was published in 2014, she was on maternity leave with their second child, Polly. It made sense for her to stay at Mikkeller, for whom she'd already written press releases. Also, they needed someone full-time to do PR and write copy.

For a long time, Mikkel Bjergsø was determined—on principle—not to spend money on advertising. On the other hand, the company now needed Pernille Pang. She understood what he wanted with Mikkeller and her education allowed her to communicate messages to the press. Also, she had developed a large network of contacts from her internship at *Politiken*. So she became the company's first press manager. Later, as the company grew, for a time she was also responsible for designing several new bars and restaurants. Today she is branding director and co-owner of Mikkeller.

While the bar on Viktoriagade was being built in 2010, the carpenter Nikolaj Eis asked one of his friends if he could help sand tables and varnish various objects. That friend, Jacob Alsing, was actually a military man, but he was ready to lend a hand. Once the bar was subsequently finished, he started frequenting it. Although initially he didn't grasp a thing about beer and had almost never drunk craft beer, he quickly became a kind of barfly at Mikkeller.

The following year, when they held the first Mikkeller Beer Celebration—then called the Copenhagen Beer Celebration—Alsing

"If you only learn about the world from what you read in books, you have no idea what it really looks like."

– Mikkel Bjergsø

Rasmus "Magic" Malmstrøm performs at a Mikkeller beer tasting aboard an SAS flight, on the occasion of the brewery and airline entering into a collaboration. For several years Malmstrøm performed magic on the floor and on stage at Mikkeller events and traveled around with the company. He even had a beer named after him: Staff Magician.

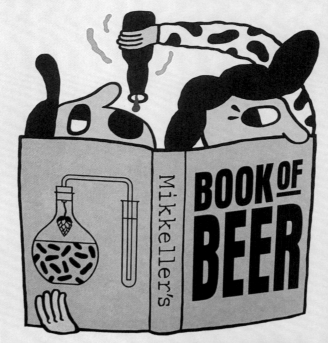

realized that help was needed at an organizational level. As far as he was concerned, his background in the army had provided certain tools on that front. So he suggested becoming a volunteer coordinator who could facilitate the purely logistical challenges. Bjergsø accepted that help enthusiastically—and even though things didn't run totally smoothly that first year, it was still better than if he hadn't been involved.

At the time, Alsing had reached a point in his life when he needed to test himself in a whole new setting. He had started serving in the Danish Army in 1993. Actually, he wanted to be a conscientious objector, but when that proved impossible, he reluctantly took a stint on Bornholm. He soon realized that he actually had a talent for the military and was sent to sergeant school. Since his poor high school record wasn't exactly opening any doors—and since he didn't really know what else to do—he applied to officer school and was also admitted there.

Jacob Alsing felt right at home in the gap between the purely practical and the very theoretical aspects of management and organization. Eventually, he became a division commander: he was stationed twice in Bosnia and once in Fayzabad in Afghanistan for seven months before becoming a teacher at the Defense Academy. For a while, he also held the title of major.

Alsing could have easily pursued a good career in the armed services, but after nineteen years, he decided he'd try his hand at something completely different. Mikkeller offered a new and exciting possibility. The beer wasn't the great attraction—in his view it might just as well be cement buckets or shirt buttons—but he thought Bjergsø was managing his brand in an inspiring way.

Actually, the two men knew each other from their childhood days growing up in Nivå. Although Alsing was a year older, he could clearly remember the twins from the area's other school who were always running. Later, when Alsing moved to Østerbro, the brothers did too; he couldn't avoid seeing them in their running clothes racing around Østerbro Stadium.

Later, when Alsing moved to Vesterbro, so did Mikkel Bjergsø. Even though they had never exchanged a word, they had many common acquaintances—so both men were aware of each other.

After the first two festivals, Mikkeller advertised a position as back office manager. At first, it was an administratively heavy role and not really suited to Jacob Alsing. He was convinced that there were others out there who would be much better at it. Still, he couldn't resist trying to kick in the door to the budding microbrewery. Therefore, he called Mikkel Bjergsø and said: "I really want to work for you—but I don't want that position. I want to be responsible for people and for operations."

At that time, Mikkeller had hired a recruitment agency to help find the right person. Mikkel Bjergsø encouraged Alsing to apply for the position anyway and even put in a few good words for him. To Alsing's great surprise, he got the job.

In that year, 2012, Mikkeller was both a large and a small business. On one hand, there were no more than four or five employees in the main office, located over a jewelry store and a Chinese restaurant on Vesterbrogade. Two employees were also working at the warehouse, where the beer was stored, and

Mikkeller's Book of Beer was published by Gyldendal in 2014. Mikkel Bjergsø's wife at the time, Pernille Pang, wrote the book in close collaboration with him. The book has since been translated into English, Swedish, Finnish, and Japanese.

a handful of workers ran the bar in Viktoriagade. On the other hand, Mikkeller regularly appeared in the top five of the best breweries in the world on RateBeer. The company, which had recently won a gold medal in the lager category for its beer American Dream, was exporting to about fifty countries worldwide.

Still, Mikkeller was experiencing growing pains, which put a strain on Mikkel Bjergsø. Since those early days of homebrewing, he'd been involved in every process, so it was difficult for him to let go. He felt trapped. Because the business was his, he had a hard time letting go of control. Yet, at the same time, the situation couldn't go on. He had less and less time to deal with the purely creative part of the business. He wanted to dedicate himself to inventing beer, developing the company, and coming up with new ideas; instead, he was swallowed up by all his administrative duties.

Therefore, hiring Jacob Alsing was like a gift from above. One by one, Alsing immediately began to take over Bjergsø's tasks. Although they were only just learning how to work together, they quickly fell into a clear hierarchy: Bjergsø finally got the space to be creative, while the Major—which quickly became Alsing's nickname—fixed what needed to be fixed. Their roles suited both men well, as they were not equal partners. Bjergsø had to remain the one who steered the ship, whereas Alsing, thanks to his strong military background, thrived in clear hierarchies.

Early on, Bjergsø set up an advisory board, which meant that Mikkeller had to face certain criticism. It was an attempt to avoid blind spots by constantly having an external review of the company by outsiders who could ask: "Have you thought about this?" Because it was an advisory board, however, Bjergsø could do whatever he wanted. At the time, he was still the sole owner, and although he sparred regularly with Jacob Alsing, the latter's role was largely not to get in the way.

Between the two of them, the distribution of roles was clear: Bjergsø did the thinking, while Jacob Alsing solved the problems. The latter was perfectly happy to stay completely out of the creative process; in his eyes, Mikkeller didn't need any more creative minds. The company's founder had a handle on that—as long as he actually had room to do so. Bjergsø had a clear picture of what Mikkeller was supposed to be. His most important function was to try to facilitate it.

Jacob Alsing's primary task was to run operations, which gave him the unofficial title of Operations Manager. Sometimes he was sent on impossible tasks. Because Mikkel Bjergsø now had a sidekick who followed orders, he could afford to be the one with the high-flying ideas. If he wanted to hold a new event, Jacob Alsing immediately set about finding locations. And if they were sitting on a plane and Bjergsø suddenly decided it would be cool to get their beer onto SAS flights, his friend's task was to make it happen.

In 2016, Mikkeller landed the large Scandinavian airline's account—becoming the first microbrewery to enter into a collaboration with an airline. In this connection, they held the world's probably highest beer tasting at an altitude of almost ten kilometers: uninitiated passengers had the opportunity to taste five of the ten beers Mikkeller had brewed exclusively for SAS.

Even though Mikkel and Jacob were wildly different, they were quite similar in one way: both men were ultra-competitive. Bjergsø wanted to create momentum, full speed ahead, because he wanted to be the best in the industry. That was right in Jacob Alsing's wheelhouse.

After they'd worked together for a little over half a year, in the spring of 2013, Mikkeller opened bar number two: Mikkeller & Friends. At first, there were Sundays on Viktoriagade when absolutely nothing happened, but for the most part, the new bar was doing really well—maybe a little too well. Before long, Bjergsø had to admit that

there was no room at all to facilitate demand. Eventually, there was a queue out into the street almost every day, and business was skyrocketing.

"We had a strong brand," says Bjergsø. "We'd received quite a lot of media coverage, and people had gotten to know the bar. There really were a lot of tourists. It had become one of the bars to visit for beer nerds, so a lot of foreign guests flew in to cross it off their checklist. Nearly ninety percent of our transactions were foreign. It was totally crazy. But that also meant that there was never any room, so not many locals came. If you have to stand in line for half an hour to get a beer, you'll just go somewhere else."

Bjergsø thought that the time was right to open a new bar. He looked at premises on

Mikkeller has produced a number of beers in collaboration with the airline SAS, including The Cloud Hopper.

Top: a label for a beer that Mikkeller made specifically for SAS.

Bottom: two posters from the collaboration, which over time has spawned around 15 different products, including organic vodka with hops. Mikkeller's SAS beers are the first brewed specifically for an airline, to help improve the quality of food and drink on planes. The beers were specially designed to function under the prevailing cabin pressure in an airplane.

When Mikkeller opened bar number two in 2013, this time on Stefansgade in Copenhagen's Nørrebro neighborhood, the company continued in the same vein with a bright Scandinavian aesthetic.

Øster Farimagsgade in the city center but ultimately chose an old recycling shop in the hip Stefansgade-quarter in Nørrebro. The space needed a certain amount of work to turn it into an inviting beer bar; they actually had to start from scratch and, among other things, cast the floor before they could even get started.

"There was seriously nothing there," he recalls. "It was just a hole in the ground with lots of moisture. But it also meant that our starting rent was cheap."

Originally, the new bar was supposed to open at the same time as the famous American microbrewery 3 Floyds Brewing Company—and then they would simultaneously open another bar together in the 3 Floyds' hometown of Chicago. None of that came to fruition. A couple of years passed before they finally put the pieces together and opened WarPigs in Vesterbro in Copenhagen.

Instead, two of Bjergsø's former students from Det Frie Gymnasium, who had founded the microbrewery To Øl (Two Beers), bought a stake in the new bar, which therefore rightly came to bear the name Mikkeller & Friends.

"The new bar was intended more for the local Copenhagen crowd. It was also supposed to take some of the pressure off opening the bar—at least, we thought it would."

For opening day in March 2013, Mikkeller had promised a thousand free beers. Actually, Bjergsø thought that number was too high, but he was about to get a shock when twice as many people showed up. All day long there were long queues into the street. They had to send visitors in through one door and out another, so they wouldn't create traffic jams when refueling from one of the forty taps featuring rotating selections of beers from all over world. People flew in from everywhere to be part of the festivities. To add a little kick to the festivities, Bjergsø had hired the Copenhagen noise rock band Ring Them Bells.

"It was a huge party, and the band played so loudly that we were banned from ever playing live music again. There were so many complaints on opening day that the landlord said we were never allowed to do that again. It was totally insane. People went crazy."

Already that same year, Mikkeller & Friends had been named the World's Best Bar on RateBeer.

More than 1,000 people turned up in 2013 for the opening of Mikkeller & Friends on Stefansgade in Nørrebro.

VI

FOR
EIGN
ADVEN
TURE

After a good fifteen minutes' drive, Johannes Jensen turns off the main road and continues instead down a bumpy gravel lane. At its end, he stops and steps out into the fresh air. The same goes for Mikkel Bjergsø and his three travel companions: Jacob Alsing, who stopped being his right-hand man in Mikkeller in August 2021 after almost ten years; Christian Tang-Jespersen, a partner in the American venture capital company ACME; and Mark Emil Hermansen, who was previously employed at Noma and is now behind the experimental spirits company Empirical, which he co-founded.

A little earlier in the day, the four Danes arrived at the Faroe Islands, where they'll spend the next three days. It's one of those trips Bjergsø has frequently cultivated in his time at Mikkeller: he can arrange the practical, take a breather, and fill the tank with new ideas, all at once.

From the lookout point on this crisp autumn day, you can see beyond Lake Leynar, which is surrounded by hills in autumn-green colors. A light haze shrouds the landscape. On the shore, consisting of black volcanic sand, there's a small black wooden hut with green moss on the roof. This is the departure point for visiting the restaurant Koks, located in a small farmhouse built in 1741, found further down by an adjacent stream. Koks is the country's only Michelin-star restaurant, which Johannes Jensen owns. In addition to a number of restaurants and bars, the country's most famous entrepreneur also owns the large Hotel Føroyar in Tórshavn. For several years, he and Bjergsø have been both partners and personal friends, and as often as the opportunity arises, the Dane jumps on a plane to go north.

In fact, Mikkel Bjergsø was recently admitted to Havneklubben, an old men's lodge on the Faroe Islands with roots dating back to 1799. He's the first person to become a member who doesn't live on the Faroe Islands. His commitment there—with his own bar, for

example—resulted in a membership. Over the years, he's encountered these kinds of special experiences thanks to opening his bars in unconventional places.

"I see it as a bit of an honor to be absorbed by the community up there," explains Bjergsø. "At one point I met Lars Løkke, who has a Faroese wife, and he became pretty damn jealous, because he also wanted to be part of that lodge. So, I said to him, 'Then you'll damn well have to earn it.'"

Many of the Danish microbreweries emerging at the beginning of the new millennium were locally based and often named after their geographical location: for example, Amager Brewery, Herslev Brewery, or Fanø Brewery. Some of them, such as Svaneke Brewery, eventually found a large market in Canada for their non-alcoholic beer—but only after establishing themselves on the home front. It was customary to start quite small and then gradually expand territory.

Mikkeller took the opposite approach. Bjergsø actually sold the company's first pallet of beer to the US. Long before most people in his home country had even heard of the company, Mikkeller was already exporting to around fifty countries around the world. The business adventure had started internationally and slowly moved back into Denmark. From focus to marketing, and from recruitment to product development, the company needed to be oriented toward the rest of the world—especially the US, where they were much more advanced when it came to beer and not least of all, craft beer.

After Mikkel Bjergsø opened those first two bars in Copenhagen, he realized that the next one needed to be located outside the country's borders. His good friend Chuck Stilphen owned a Belgian-style beer bar called The Trappist in Oakland, near San Francisco. Bjergsø visited the bar regularly whenever he was in that area, and the American bar

Mikkeller's first foreign bar found its home in San Francisco's gritty Tenderloin neighborhood, known for its street art and hipsters—but also for its crime and numerous homeless people.

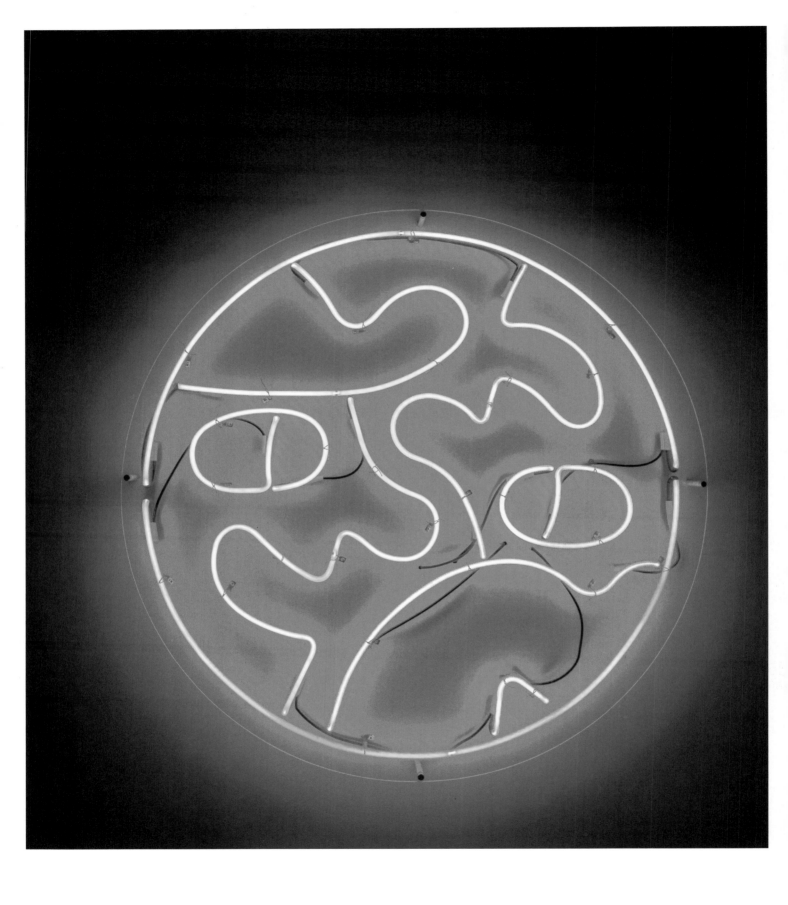

owner always visited Mikkeller when he was in Copenhagen.

During one of those visits, on a rainy night in the Danish capital, the two friends suddenly got the idea to open a bar together in San Francisco. Before the evening's close, they'd made their decision. Afterwards, Bjergsø traveled several times to the American West Coast, so they could scout locations together. Eventually, they found the perfect spot in the Tenderloin, close to Union Square in the Golden City—not the most likely place to open a bar. Sure, the neighborhood was known for street art and hip eateries, but it was particularly notorious for its many homeless people, drawn to the city by its temperate weather and thus better conditions for sleeping on the street.

"It's a wild place, but for us it was about choosing a location not everyone would just come to," notes Bjergsø. "Just like the bar on Viktoriagade. We thought we'd ensured that it wouldn't become too touristy or too much like Strøget. Still, maybe it was *just* wild enough that murders had been committed outside, crack is being smoked on the street corners, and for a long time there was a rock club next door. It's pretty rough, and even today people still comment, 'What the hell kind of place is this to put a bar?' Yet, at the same time, it also helps that many people think it's really cool."

For the new Mikkeller bar, Bjergsø once again took his starting point in the design and aesthetics of the bar on Viktoriagade. For both cultural and practical reasons, however, certain aspects had to be adjusted. In San Francisco, earthquake protection is mandatory in all buildings; in this case, that meant large metal pillars were installed in the middle of the space to prevent the whole thing from collapsing.

"On that front, it's not like a typical Mikkeller bar," observes Bjergsø. "There's a kitchen too, otherwise people won't come. It's not in the culture to just go out and drink beer. It's actually quite unique to Denmark that people eat first and then go out to drink beer. Even in neighboring Sweden and Norway, people prefer being able to get both in the same place."

At that point, the new bar was clearly the largest of all three Mikkeller bars. It had room for 42 taps, including two kegs, as well as the so-called Tivoli Sour Room in the basement, with bottled beer for sale. Mikkel Bjergsø and Chuck Stilphen had even acquired the advanced Flux Capacitor system—at that time making the bar only the fourth in the world that could control temperature and nitrogen and carbon dioxide content for each individual draft beer.

Aesthetically, the partners employed the same turquoise color as the one found in Mikkeller & Friends in Nørrebro. Certain elements had to be adapted, however, to the American location. Bjergsø learned another hard lesson when Mikkeller opened a bar, a brewery and a tasting room a year later in San Diego, a little further south in California. For the Danish bars, the design studio Femmes Régionales had chosen bar stools with wooden legs in a classic, minimalist Scandinavian style. They were keen to use the same chairs in the US. Before long, however, half of them had broken, so they had to choose something a little heavier and more industrial, which was customary on the other side of the Atlantic.

"Americans often weigh more than Europeans, so that alone places other demands on the design. You can't create a bright, feminine bar in the same way, because Americans are just, well, Americans. But as far as possible, we've used the bar on Viktoriagade as our starting point when creating bars abroad. That's our first bar—that's our identity—and that's how I would like Mikkeller to be represented."

Neon sign from Mikkeller's brewery and tasting room in Miramar in San Diego, which opened in 2015.

A little later in the day, the sun slowly dissolves the white clouds in the pale blue sky above the capital of Tórshavn. Inside a large dark-blue building, a group of workers in helmets, with reflectors on their trousers, walk around in front of some large stainless-steel tanks. From the windows above, the penetrating afternoon light casts an orangey glow across the gray concrete floor, where there are black tire tracks and pallets everywhere. A sign at the entrance reads "OY Brewing," an abbreviation for *Oyggjar*, the Faroese word for "islands."

Although Bjergsø isn't directly involved in the brewery, which will function as a brewpub restaurant, and music venue, he has promised to help Johannes Jensen and the other investors. Along the way, he helped them find equipment and brewers, and he's contributed recipes and done some branding—even though the new brewpub might become a competitor to Mikkeller's own bar in Tórshavn, which opened in 2017.

"It's a great project and I want to help Johannes," he says. "At the same time, the beer culture is still so underdeveloped there that I think it will be good if the brewery helps more people learn more about beer. Then there will be more people at our bar, too."

This afternoon, he walks around the room and does an inspection with the experienced Faroese beer king, Petur Petersen, hired to run the brewery, which will open during 2022.

The Dane nods a few times, and then says: "It's going to be fucking awesome."

The next day, Bjergsø and the rest of the group, led by Johannes Jensen, tour the majestic landscape with its large open fells and broad lakes. A river slices through the green landscape, and a rainbow suddenly illuminates four sheep in their respective colors walking across the field. Low clouds erase the environs and then lighten to reveal rocky islands on the horizon.

The evening sun casts shadows from the tall cliffs, hardened by the waves over millions

"If I opened bars purely for business reasons, I'd have never chosen Bangkok— or Warsaw, Bucharest, or Tórshavn, for that matter."

– Mikkel Bjergsø

Mikkel Bjergsø, who has always had a soft spot for the Faroe Islands, visits the country as often as he can.

Mikkeller's bar in Tórshavn on the Faroe Islands is housed in a 400-year-old wooden building.

of years, glistening in the surface of the open sea, where an older man in orange waders and a black cap sails a white cutter through the windy weather.

As darkness has long since fallen, Mikkel Bjergsø and the others show up at a more than four-hundred-year-old wooden house in the capital's historic quarter, tucked away among pristine fjords and surrounded by free-ranging sheep. Inside the light-brown building with its wooden ceiling beams and sod roof, the place is almost full. The local bartender has to constantly pour a new beer from one of the sixteen taps carrying both Mikkeller and beer brewed by friends from near and far.

About 13,000 people live in Tórshavn, making it Europe's smallest capital. Selling alcohol in the country was illegal until 1992. Still, Mikkel Bjergsø has always been driven by his desire to open bars in the most unique

The bar in Tórshavn, one of Mikkeller's most unique locations, is located in a small cluster of houses with grass roofs in the city center, with the harbor just around the corner. When the bar opened, it was inaugurated with locals and people from Mikkeller, all of whom folk-danced hand in hand through all the houses.

Mikkeller

BANGKOK

places. He says it only makes sense when your ambition is to create unique beers.

Mikkel Bjergsø met Pernille Pang, the mother of his two daughters, around 2000 (they remained a couple until 2019). Shortly after they met, the pair spent three months traveling around Asia. They landed in Thailand—and although Bjergsø had never been there, the place made an indelible impression on him. Their eldest daughter, Stella, was born a few years later. They took her to Asia when she was no more than nine months old, and since then the family has been there frequently.

"I love everything about Thailand," he says, "the climate, the food, the people. Everything about it is awesome. You can sit at a street kitchen in Bangkok and eat something outrageously delicious for a dollar or less. It's hard to find a cooler place to take a vacation."

Thus, Bjergsø had no doubts about where to plant the next flag in the carefully growing empire. He met a Danish guy, a resident of Thailand who was importing

Mikkeller's beer into the country, and after visiting a few times, they agreed to open a bar in the capital city of Bangkok.

"There were zero beer bars in Bangkok—and craft beer was almost non-existent," explains Bjergsø. "So, it wasn't exactly the most obvious place to open a bar. But at the same time, that's what appealed to me, because the possibility was there to try to change something."

At that time, the microbrewery scene was virtually nonexistent in Thailand. Both locals and thousands of tourists drank only Singha and Chang, the cheapest beers on the market. Instead of trying to establish himself in the chaos of the capital's touristy and vibrant main street, Sukhumvit (famous *and* infamous for its numerous side streets with strip clubs, prostitution, etc.), Bjergsø repeated the now well-known formula and instead found the perfect location in a local residential area.

"If you open in a touristy area in Thailand, tons of tourists will come barreling in expecting strip bars, naked women, and stuff like that—and they were not the type of guests I was looking for," he says.

On the recommendation of his Danish business partner in the country, he found his way to the Ekkamai district, an area where many local Thais frequent restaurants and coffee shops. Mikkeller opened there in an old Thai house from the 1950s. You have to enter through a garden gate and proceed through the tropical garden with beanbag chairs out front before reaching the bar with its very large glass windows. The location was perfect.

"The only problem was that no one could find the damn bar," admits Bjergsø. "When I'd get into a taxi in Bangkok and try to explain where we needed to go, no one had any idea what I was talking about."

Eventually, Bjergsø applied to the authorities in Thailand to have official Mikkeller signs made to guide people in the right direction. Another boost to the bar's reputation came when the restaurant Upstairs by Mikkeller opened on the first floor, in collaboration with Dan Fey. The Korean chef had worked in various restaurants in Bangkok but wanted to open his own place. Since he was already enthusiastic about Mikkeller, they decided to put the pieces together. His wife took care of the hostess duties, and he took care of the menu, which included spicy chicken wings in Szechuan sauce and the popular Mikkeller Wagyu Burger with cheddar, sautéed mushrooms, and a juicy wagyu steak. Before long, they were acknowledged for all of it with a Michelin star.

"At that point there were absolutely no restaurants with Michelin stars in Thailand," explains Bjergsø. "In fact, in Asia, that had only happened in Japan and Singapore—but we managed to get a star in our very first year."

Of course, that also meant that Upstairs by Mikkeller quickly gained a well-known reputation among the city's finer citizens. The rich and famous began to make their way to the old villa in Ekkamai, where they encountered something a little different than they were used to. In Thailand, most fine restaurants are located in five-star hotels, but here they first had to go through a garden, where people were lounging around and drinking craft beer, and then further in through the beer bar and up a flight of stairs in the middle of the locale.

"It was a bit of a culture shock for the celebrities there. They were accustomed to getting the red carpet, but suddenly found themselves in the middle of a beer bar. It was really funny—but it worked."

Right from the start, Mikkel Bjergsø knew that the bar in Thailand would probably never be any great money-maker for Mikkeller.

"If I opened bars purely for business reasons, I'd never have chosen Bangkok—or Warsaw, Bucharest, or Tórshavn, for that matter," comments Bjergsø. "It's much more to do with personal reasons, a way to build the brand so that you also get to know it better. It hasn't been driven at all by any business plan. I love to travel and visit new places, and it's just been cool to get the brand out into the world that way. Mikkeller was the first modern microbrewery to open a bar in Asia."

Business played a somewhat larger role, however, in the opening of the bar in San Francisco. Still, even to this day, that bar has earned the most money over the years; in fact, among all of Mikkeller's pubs, only WarPigs in Copenhagen has done better. Already on opening day in 2013, there was a lot of hype, with the BBC making its way through the Tenderloin. At the same time, Bjergsø's twin brother, Jeppe Jarnit-Bjergsø, opened his first bar in New York—and the media quickly picked up on it. So the two brothers who had each conquered an American coast were soon in the press.

"From the start we had a good brand—but this helped to create a lot of media buzz. In almost record time, it put Mikkeller on the map."

The outdoor garden of Mikkeller's bar in the hip Ekkamai neighborhood of Bangkok, Thailand.

VII

END LESS COMPETI TION

Jeppe was supposed to be born first. Had everything gone as planned, he would have been pushed out first to see the light of day, and then Mikkel would have come next. But that's not the way it went, because Mikkel was in the wrong position, making a Caesarian section necessary. Therefore, he came into the world first on September 15, 1975—a minute and a half before his twin brother.

Their mother, Sonja Bjergsø, discovered she was expecting twins two months before her due date. She had grown huge during her pregnancy; at the same time there was an unusual amount of activity in her stomach, so she was sent to a doctor to be examined. They still found only one heartbeat, yet there were two spines. That was unusual. Because the doctors were worried that she'd give birth prematurely, with potentially dire consequences, she was hospitalized. She spent the rest of her pregnancy at Øresund Hospital in Copenhagen.

That summer, Denmark had a heat wave that proved to be one of its hottest. A record was set on August 10, when the thermometer hit 36.4 degrees Celsius (94.5 degrees Fahrenheit). While a pregnant Sonja Bjergsø was lying in the hospital room and sweating, she passed the time knitting, reading crime novels, and listening to records by the Doors, Bob Dylan, and the Beatles. Her boyfriend, Jens Borg Nielsen, stopped by often to keep her company.

Sonja was an office assistant, and Jens was a lawyer who worked as a deputy inspector in Vestre Prison. They'd met each other two years earlier in the penal system, where they both worked. The couple came from very different backgrounds: she was the daughter of a shoemaker on Amager, while he came from a wealthy family in Tårbæk, the son of an executive at the Danish chocolatier Anthon Berg. Both parents already had one child of their own—and now they were about to become parents again, this time together, to twins.

The couple had a lot to be happy about, but doctors' concerns were putting a damper on their joy. With identical twins in the same amnion, and sharing the same placenta, each with his own umbilical cord, the birth could be complicated. Especially since one of the twins was lying in the wrong position. When it became clear that it was impossible to turn him around, they initiated a so-called breech birth; but Sonja Bjergsø had contractions and didn't open sufficiently. That only made the situation even more critical, because there was a risk that child number two wouldn't survive.

Instead, the doctors had to perform a Caesarean section, which meant that Mikkel was the first to see the light of day (at around one pm, on September 15, 1975). If it had been a normal birth, Jeppe would have been born first. When the latter was confronted with that fact many years later in a popular article in the *New York Times,* he replied, "I usually say he created problems for me even before we were born."

No one could ever have predicted that the newborn twin boys would one day revolutionize the beer industry, and yet destroy their interpersonal relationship in a way that would make headlines around the world. Mikkel and Jeppe grew up in a rowhouse on Fasanvænget in Kokkedal. Their half-brother came to visit every other weekend, whereas their half-sister only showed up at Christmas at their grandparents' house. The twins' parents were pretty left-leaning, which was not exactly uncommon in the 1970s. Their mother wore bellbottoms, the father was into jazz, and when the children were particularly lucky, they had chicken with French fries on Saturday. Otherwise, they went into Copenhagen to eat at a Pakistani restaurant, which the parents really enjoyed.

The family traveled several times to Greece for their summer vacation. Only few people could do so back then, but their father's job as a prison inspector provided a few more luxuries. Their mother had a special sense for aesthetics, so there were both a Børge Mogensen sofa and a Verner Panton chair in the home. The living room often served as the setting for festive gatherings, where ashtrays, scattered all around the dining room table, were filled and where the Danish beers Hof, Tuborg, and Faxe Fad were served in their characteristic small, chubby bottles. Although the parents liked beer, they weren't exactly beer nerds. The nearest they came to that world was described in the book *Beer Brothers:* "… on special occasions they went to the pub Bernikow, in inner Copenhagen, where they had a half and half—that is, half porter and half pilsner."

In the quiet neighborhood around their rowhouse in Kokkedal, Mikkel and Jeppe spent most of their time doing boyish pranks—which they were both pretty good at. They had their favorites: for example, they'd stuff poop in a plastic bag, put it on a random doorstep, and then set fire to it. Then they'd ring the doorbell and scurry off to seek refuge. When some innocent resident opened the door and saw that something burning, their automatic response was to step on it, and thus on the shit. At other times, they'd smear door handles with butter or put thumbtacks on the bike path and then hide in bushes nearby so they could watch as people punctured their tires. They weren't exactly troublemakers, but they were wild boys who liked to stir things up. According to Mikkel, Jeppe was often a little wilder and more transgressive. Still, they were connected, because they were each other's best friends and inseparable.

Because the twins were the spitting image of each other, people had trouble telling them apart as soon as they stepped outside the house. Even their half-brother, Kasper, who lived with his mother, couldn't tell them apart when he came to visit every other weekend. Instead, people began to refer to the twins as one entity, as if they were only one person. At times, that could be advantageous, as when they made fools out of their

teachers at school by pretending to be each other. Yet maybe that also laid the groundwork for the two boys doing everything they could to stand out from each other.

"As identical twins, you're constantly compared to each other," observes Mikkel Bjergsø. "Everyone viewed us as one person and they would talk about us in the plural. 'Now they've done it again.' I found it totally annoying."

The brothers began to compete constantly, each one trying to surpass the other in just about every conceivable discipline. Early on, they tried their hand at soccer. Although both twins were fast, they weren't particularly adroit with the ball—so they both lost interest. The same thing happened with table tennis and then boy scouts. Who wanted to stand around whittling branches and tying strings? Their mutual competition craved a little more momentum, so instead it took other, more atypical forms: bicycle races, emptying the dishwasher the fastest, or cleaning out the candy bowl in the shortest time.

Still, even though they quarreled—and sometimes even fought—they were each other's best friends, allies who had each other's back. As long as it was the two of them, they could handle anything. They became conscious of this bond when, as eight-year-olds, they were called into the living room and told that their parents were getting a divorce. Even though they'd definitely seen them quarrel, it still shocked both of them, who let the tears run freely.

"I can still vividly remember when we got the news," recalls Bjergsø. "It definitely had a profound effect on me."

Their father had met someone else and soon moved to North Jutland, where he got a job in another prison and started a new family. The twins stayed with their mother, who tried to manage them and the family's suddenly tight household budget.

"Sometimes we'd visit our father, but it never went well. We always felt a little beside ourselves. He had a new child, and we

Mikkel Bjergsø and his twin brother, Jeppe, in the garden of their child-hood home in Nivå.

no longer felt like his first priority," explains Bjergsø.

In time, they stopped visiting their father altogether. Sometimes he'd send gifts in an attempt to still be part of their lives, but that was the only contact they had with him for many years. For Mikkel and Jeppe, on the other hand, their parents' break-up only pushed them even closer. They had each other, so everything else was less important.

As they got older, however, the competition between them also heightened. As eleven-year-olds, both twins started running middle-distance races. They were good—and having someone they always wanted to beat only made them better. When they competed in the 800-meter race at the Aarhus Games

athletics competition in 1994, both twins ran their best race ever. As Mikkel crossed the finish line, the toe of the shoe was only one-hundredth of a second ahead of Jeppe's.

"We hung around together all the time and always trained together. We got a lot out of being each other's training partner, because we were at roughly the same level. If I didn't win, I'd hope that Jeppe won, because it was better than coming in third," says Bjergsø.

They were thick as thieves. One would enter a room to say something, and the other would come in shortly thereafter and say the exact same thing. When they were in the right mood, they were great company—and then their circle of friends found them both fun and comfortable to be with. But they had a rather complicated relationship, which Pernille

Left: Mikkel Bjergsø and his twin brother, Jeppe, in a fierce battle during an athletics competition.

Right: the twins photographed with their mother, Sonja.

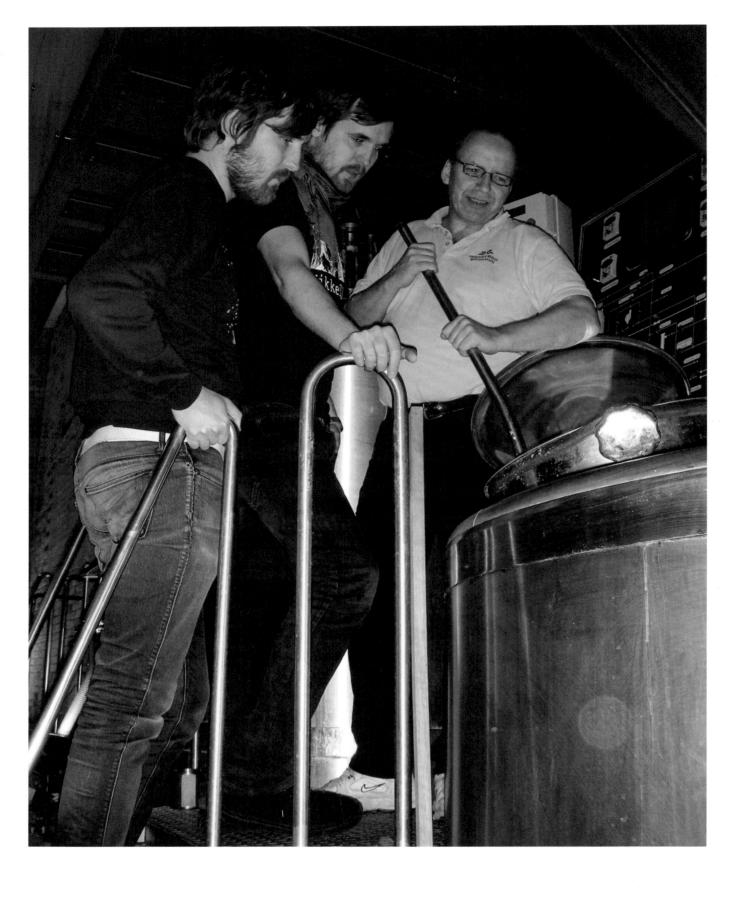

discovered when she and Mikkel became lovers. In her own family background, she wasn't used to such wide mood swings. Therefore, she found it remarkable when at any given moment the twins could become such enemies that they both stormed off in anger. Yet, as quickly as tempers flared up, just as suddenly it would be over—and then they were good friends again.

After practicing high-level elite running in their teens, both twins became schoolteachers in their twenties before entering the beer world almost simultaneously. At this time the now world-famous feud really took root. The unbreakable bond of childhood was replaced with a frosty, conflict-filled relationship. In 2014, the *New York Times* published a long article entitled "A Fight is Brewing" about the identical twins on each side of the Atlantic building their respective microbrewery empires who couldn't stand each other.

The media has frequently speculated about when the conflict originated. Some believe it started when Mikkel Bjergsø opened his first Mikkeller beer bar in Viktoriagade in Copenhagen, in 2010. A few years earlier, Jeppe Jarnit-Bjergsø had opened his own beer shop—where his twin brother had delivered beer—but now they went from being allies to competing in the burgeoning market. Thomas Schøn, Mikkeller's first employee, explained to the *New York Times* that it created friction in the brothers' relationship: "Their relationship began to fall apart."

That same year, Jeppe founded his own brewery—Evil Twin Brewing—and the two brothers were now official competitors. At least that's how he saw it, as he explained in the same article: "Mikkeller had always been the brand in my store, so when Mikkel opened his bar, I said, 'If he doesn't want to do it for me, then I'll just do it for myself.'"

"You don't understand what it means to be a twin if you aren't one. If Jeppe hurt himself as a child, it hurt me almost as much."

– Mikkel Bjergsø

The twin brothers during a brewing at Nørrebro Bryghus in 2007.

Others feel that the brothers' conflict has less to do with any specific event and far more to do with their respective personalities. They might be similar as two drops of water, but they differ on several fronts. Mikkel is often described as reserved, whereas Jeppe is more outgoing, more sociable, and wilder. He's also viewed as more uncertain, if you believe their mutual childhood friend, Kristian Keller. In the *New York Times* article, Keller describes Jeppe as someone with a greater need to prove his worth, the reason he talks so much, while Mikkel, on the other hand, doesn't waste his time trying to get people to like him.

There are also those who think that the whole conflict is actually a calculated marketing stunt, a story so good the media can't avoid it, creating attention for their common good. However, both twins have rejected this idea on numerous occasions. Before Jeppe moved to New York, the two brothers actually tried to reconcile with a form of couples therapy; that lasted for several months, without bearing any fruit. Since then, Jeppe has described how he opened up and let the tears flow without triggering any reaction from his twin. Conversely, Mikkel didn't see it that way—he believed *he* was the one who'd made the effort as far as attempting to find some reconciliation. Back in 2014, he reportedly wrote an email in which he tried to bury the hatchet, which came to nothing. That same year, he also sent Jeppe an invitation to his newly initiated, annual beer festival in Copenhagen, where he wanted to gather microbreweries around the world, but his twin brother canceled at the last minute.

Undoubtedly, their relationship became increasingly difficult with time. Eventually, the two brothers could no longer stand to be in the same room—and if they had to be, they simply didn't talk to each other. Somehow, there was no real room for both of them. In 2012, Jeppe moved to New York, where he turned Evil Twin Brewing into a physical brewery and opened a bar, Tørst, in Greenpoint, Brooklyn.

Since then, Jeppe's brewery has also expanded. By 2019, Evil Twin was selling beer in thirty-five states in the United States, with exports to more than 35 different countries. Like his twin brother, he has experimented wildly, producing beer with such ingredients as blueberries, lemon peel, oak, cocoa, chocolate, coconut, cinnamon, chili, coffee, vanilla, chestnut, and marshmallows. Jeppe has garnered an excellent reputation on the international microbrewery scene, where he has even helped the renowned Danish Michelin-star restaurant Noma select beer.

When Jeppe Jarnit-Bjergsø traveled across the Atlantic about ten years ago, he wasn't only saying good-bye to Denmark—he was also saying good-bye to his twin brother. Except for a single time, when Mikkel Bjergsø and his family visited Jeppe and his family shortly after they moved, and at a wedding with mutual acquaintances, the two brothers haven't seen each other.

Mikkel Bjergsø did reestablish contact with his father, however, in the early 2000s. His older half-brother initiated it. Although Mikkel still felt some anger and resentment from his childhood, they managed to revive their relationship. As it turned out, his father was also into beer and had a cellar with about four hundred different brews that he'd collected over the years. That impressed Mikkel—so when he opened his first bar on Viktoriagade, he invited his father too, the first time his parents were together since his childhood. They didn't return immediately to a classic father-son relationship, but they stayed in touch and the relationship between grandfather and Mikkel's two daugthers was important for both Mikkel and his father.

At the time they reestablished contact, eighteen years had passed, and Mikkel had long since accepted the fact that his father wasn't a part of his life. At least that's what he believed. For long periods of time, he didn't think about his father, yet he was well aware that something might still be smoldering. Bjergsø is no stranger to the classic tale of the successful man longing for recognition from his father. You're never good enough, because you're not getting recognition from the most important person. Therefore, you push on, constantly striving for new achievements. Still, was that the impetus for his own inner drive—or was it the potent combination of a twin brother to compete with and an absent father whose recognition he'd longed for?

"I'm not naïve. I know what it means when something gets into your head. You want to prove to your father that you're good enough, because, naturally, we felt betrayed. But I never thought that was the reason for my competitive nature or my need to create something. I've always associated it with the fact that I'm an identical twin."

Mikkel Bjergsø isn't the only one who sees it that way. For years now, he's had to live with the fact that the conflict with his twin has become part of the public narrative about both himself and Mikkeller. The sensational story has found its way into numerous international media. The production company AMC Entertainment, which is behind such successful series as *Breaking Bad*, *Mad Men*, and *The Walking Dead*, has even tried in vain to make a TV series about the twins' lives.

Even though Bjergsø knows the name of the game—conflict sells newspapers—he finds the press's infatuation with his chilly relationship with his brother totally ridiculous. At several times over the years, the beer industry's infamous cold war seemed to be thawing. For example, at one point, Mikkeller and Evil Twin Brewing launched a beer in "collaboration" with the American brewery Jolly Pumpkin. As it turned out, however, Jolly Pumpkin's owner Ron Jeffries, a friend of both brothers, had simply been a bit too cunning and launched the beer—a mix of the three breweries—without either twin knowing the other was involved.

Over the years, Mikkel Bjergsø has avoided the subject frequently, whenever yet another journalist asks him to explain the situation between him and Jeppe. How can he explain it to someone who would never understand it anyway?

"You can't understand what it means to be a twin if you aren't one," explains Bjergsø. "If Jeppe hurt himself as a child, it hurt me almost as much. There was actual physical discomfort to it. You share a different bond with a person you can totally see yourself reflected in—who looks like you, thinks like you, feels like you, and often does the same things as you. You almost speak the same language, one that no one else understands."

Even though Mikkel Bjergsø no longer holds out any hope of a reconciliation, he still wishes the situation were different. As he says, this isn't how it ends for *all* identical twins.

"The bond I've always felt with Jeppe is completely broken. I've accepted that this is how it is, and I no longer feel as if I'm missing a part of myself. But I think it's totally insane that I can run into a human being who is my spitting image—and who I have nothing at all to do with. I wish he would come to Copenhagen one day, and we could meet for a beer and say, 'Fuck, man, how cool is it that we are both doing so well?'"

VIII

HENRY & SALLY

In the mornings, when Keith Shore steps out his front door in his hometown of Philadelphia, he doesn't have to take more than twenty steps before he shows up for work. Shore has his own small studio in the backyard, about half an hour north of the city center. There's just enough space for two desks, so that Mikkeller's graphic designer, Luke Cloran, has somewhere to sit when he arrives during the week (as he did before Covid-19). To one side, there's a wide view of nature, where foxes and deer run wild while birds chirp. Unless the neighbors are using their lawn mowers, windows stay open so that the sounds of nature permeate, along with the fresh suburban air.

Since 2013, Shore has been Mikkeller's art director—and for most people, his ingenious labels spring to mind whenever anyone mentions the Danish microbrewery. In fact, it was pure coincidence that initially brought him and Mikkel Bjergsø together more than twelve years ago. At the time, Shore had been working as a freelance illustrator for ten years. Along the way, his designs included myriad projects: magazines, skateboards, book covers, and clothes. His philosophy had always been to take on as many different—and fun— projects as possible. One day he walked into a bottle shop in New Jersey, where he was living, and suddenly noticed an old bottle on top of one of the shelves. The raw, hand-drawn logo piqued his interest.

"Back then, it was quite rare to see a really beautiful beer or wine bottle," says Shore. "So it caught my eye."

At that time the beer scene was much different. Although he'd done a lot of work, the thought of doing designs and illustrations for that industry had never crossed his mind. After he saw the old beer bottle on the shelf, however, and figured out it belonged to Mikkeller, he found the Danish microbrewery's home page and sent an email directly to the man who ran it.

A reply came shortly thereafter, and the two men started writing back and forth.

Keith Shore sent some of his drawings. When Mikkel Bjergsø happened to be at an event in West Philly, not long afterward, they met in person. They agreed that the American illustrator should design the label for the beer I Hardcore You, a collab between Mikkeller and the Scottish brewery BrewDog. Since no concrete job description existed, he simply drew what he found fun and interesting.

"It was cool to see people drinking something that had your art on the label," observes Shore. "I've always drawn very small—it really fits my style—so I was quite comfortable with it. I loved every second, and afterwards I begged Mikkel to let me do it again."

That resulted in yet another assignment. This time, Shore used two characters with octagonal faces who had sprung to life in his sketchbooks a few months earlier: Henry & Sally, who since then have become synonymous with Mikkeller's beer.

Once upon a time, beer was viewed as something only old men imbibed. How it tasted wasn't really that important—and certainly not how it was packaged. That was evident on the numerous labels conjuring up images of Chesterfield sofas and sporting events on TV screens. That's far from the case now, and the change can be ascribed to the revolution in microbrewery with its myriad labels on bottles and cans, small artworks in and of themselves.

As a child, Keith Shore loved serial comics like *Mad Magazine*. When he got older, his heroes were Philip Guston, David Hockney, and Henri Matisse—all of whom helped to mold him as an artist. Those influences became evident in his illustrations and colorful cartoon figures, who are subtle yet also aesthetic.

Shore's approach spoke directly to Mikkel Bjergsø's desire to change the beer industry. Although he was interested in finding a common motif, he wasn't interested in drinking good beer out of ugly bottles. Whereas

recognizable beer labels were often dull, as
if they were adhering to a format, Mikkeller's
dynamic universe found proper expression
and the right visual identity in Keith Shore's
almost naïve approach to creating cartoon
characters with clear contours.

Because Bjergsø was full speed ahead
with Mikkeller, he had no time for any involved
communication or sparring and back and forth
with an artist. Therefore, finding an American
illustrator who didn't need to deliver a big
presentation—one who could just get started—was a perfect fit.

"Mikkel always says, 'You're the artist,
not me.' Just as I could never dream of telling
him how to make beer, he never gets in the
way of the creative process. He really lets me
do my thing. It's a dream for all artists, and
that's probably the main reason why I've been
there so long."

Keith Shore wasn't employed by Mikkeller
for long when—in connection with an art
exhibition—he brought drawings of the two

The first label Art Director Keith
Shore designed for Mikkeller was
for the beer I Hardcore You, a collaboration with the Scottish brewery BrewDog.

119

characters he'd begun to portray more frequently on various labels. In that regard, he thought it would be a good idea to name them. Therefore, the man with the hat was called Henry, and the woman with the big hair became Sally. Since then, he's told the story of the two hop-sniffing, long-nosed partners in small fragments on each label.

"If you see a big hat and a big nose, you immediately think of Mikkeller. It's fantastic that people buy into the brand that way. Of course, it's always been important to me that my labels are fun to look at—but the most important thing is that they stand out together. If you walk into a beer shop and there are ten Mikkeller beers, hopefully you'll feel that they belong together. The industry has grown ridiculously, and the beer world is very crowded. So it's important that the design is recognizable and stands out."

In Keith Shore's view, a good label will make a potential customer stop and stare—it might even make you want to turn the bottle or can over to get the whole story. Ultimately, a good label should make you open it and drink the contents.

To Shore, his primary task is to reinforce the experience of drinking what is inside. As a rule, he gets a bit of general information about each beer in advance: its style, alcohol content, format, and name. For the first few years, he asked a lot about whatever beer he had to design a label for, its ingredients, etc. As the number of beers increased, however, and he suddenly started sending over 100 beers out a year, he could no longer capture the essence of each one in advance. Instead, the process increasingly reversed, and he became the one who christened each beer from his drawings. On the whole, he has almost complete creative freedom in the design process.

"A lot of it has to do with freedom," says Shore. "They've let me explore my own process and interests. When you do something creative, you should be able to enjoy it—and I've done that. They've always been open

"If you see a big hat and a big nose, you immediately think of Mikkeller. It's fantastic that people buy into the brand that way."

– Keith Shore

After Keith Shore visited Mikkel Bjergsø and Pernille Pang at their summer house in North Zealand, he had a similar annex, which serves as his studio, built in his own backyard in Philadelphia on the US East Coast.

to letting my style evolve, to letting me take chances along the way. Often, Mikkel doesn't even see a label before he holds the beer in his hand."

Since Shore became Mikkeller's art director, his work has seen three major shifts in style. The first labels consisted of very raw pencil drawings. Later they became more collage-like, layered and photoshopped. Today, his style is, in his words, more graphic. That's occurred partially by necessity: while he previously designed maybe ten to twenty labels in a year, he and Luke now create more than 200.

"We've developed a style so we can work a little more effectively and quickly," he explains. "In the old days, I'd work on some labels for ten to fifteen hours. We no longer have that luxury. Many people who don't create their own art believe that more time equals better quality. I don't believe that at all. You can make something amazing in thirty hours or in one hour. What I've spent the most time on has rarely been the best."

Naturally, Shore has found it challenging to keep up with the brand's growth in his small backyard studio. There are no quiet days, and sometimes he's working on ten to twenty labels at a time. In addition, he's usually involved in at least a few other more atypical projects, such as collaborating with musicians, chefs, clothing designers, airlines, and whatever else has come up over the years. In the process, he has learned to trust his gut feeling, because his first idea is often the best.

"The characters of Henry and Sally made everything easier," explains Shore, "because every label has a starting point. There's always something to build on. The brand itself has become the story of these two characters and their relationship and adventure."

Keith Shore creates a mural at a pop-up bar in Portland, Oregon, on the US West Coast.

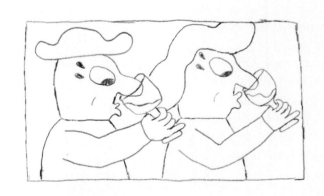

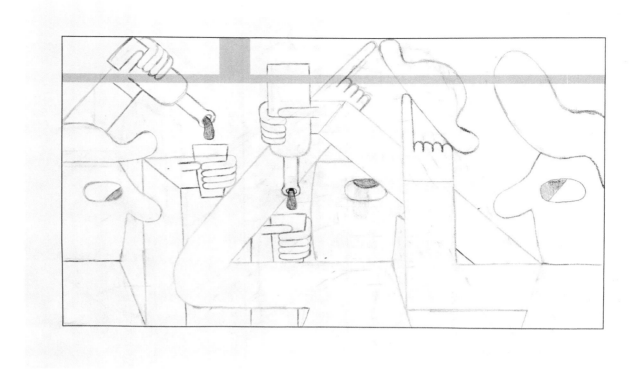

HENRY AND HIS SISTERS

A selection of Keith Shore's sketches. Over time, Shore's two characters Henry & Sally have developed into Mikkeller's mascot, featured on logos as well as labels, merchandise, and in the decor of Mikkeller's bars and restaurants.

From sketch to finished label for the beer Mikkeller Mission Chinese Food. For many years, Mikkel Bjergsø visited the Mission Chinese Food restaurant whenever he was in San Francisco. Eventually, he and the restaurant entered into a collaboration that resulted in Mikkeller opening its own branch of the restaurant in Copenhagen called Vesterbro Chinese Food.

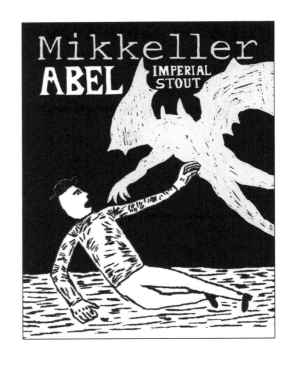

128   VIII. Henry & Sally

130   VIII. Henry & Sally

Various labels and posters created by Keith Shore. Mikkeller has become famous for entering into myriad collaborations. A number of them appear on page 132-133.

From top left: two beers made with musician Rick Astley. Help for the Danish Refugee Council. Irma. The beers Windy Hill and Raspberry Blush. The beer Japanese Rice Lager. A collaboration with Burger King. A bottled beer for the classic German brewery Uerige. The band The National. Marietta Red, made in collaboration with film director David Lynch as a tribute to the film *Wild at Heart*. Finally, three versions of Mikkeller Sparkling Water—some of Keith Shore's favorite designs.

Viktoriagade, in Copenhagen's Vesterbro neighborhood, has a special place in Mikkeller's history. At one time, the company had as many as four locations on the street: Øl & Brød, Hyggestund, Vesterbro Chinese Food, and Mikkeller Bar. In the photo, Keith Shore is painting the famous heart sculpture in connection with Mikkeller Beer Celebration Copenhagen.

IX

FULL SPEED AHEAD

For a long time, getting Mikkeller into Roskilde Festival was high on Jacob Alsing's to-do list. Mikkel Bjergsø really wanted the beer represented at Denmark's largest festival—a goal of his ever since the microbrewery's infancy. Having been a guest at the festival for many years, he'd seen food selection constantly improving over the years, but the same couldn't be said for beer. As the main sponsor, Carlsberg was everywhere; because the big beer brands almost always sponsored these festivals, they also dominated them. Bjergsø found that frustrating, because, to him, Mikkeller and microbrewery in general were part of the same culture as festivals. Obviously, they needed to become part of that culture.

"I think it was a shame that guests were basically forced to buy one product," observes Bjergsø. "It was like being able to only get a Big Mac at the festival. That would never work, so I had a hard time understanding why people just accepted the fact that they could only get Tuborg beer. I know they put a lot of money into it, but it's still crazy not to let anyone else in."

For several years, Bjergsø tried to dialogue with the organizers of Denmark's largest festival to get Mikkeller in through the back door. Because the festival's revenues were charitable, he said the microbrewery's revenue would also go to charity. One year, the organizers actually agreed to let Mikkeller set up a smaller booth—and then abruptly changed their mind, saying it couldn't be done. There was no justification for the change in attitude, although Bjergsø soon ascertained that some main sponsors probably had a hand in it.

Instead, Bjergsø employed some unusual methods. One year, Mikkeller drove a truckload of 30,000 cans of beers to Roskilde and handed them out to festival guests in front of the event. While that created a certain amount of attention, it still wasn't the real thing. Bjergsø had to admit that becoming an integral part of the festival simply wasn't possible. Tuborg had too much control.

One day, he had a revelation: "We'll just have to make our own damn festival." Knowing it would be his biggest task to date, Jacob Alsing looked at his business partner and nodded.

Over the years, Bjergsø was contacted several times by investors—from private equity funds to large breweries—wanting either to invest in Mikkeller or to buy the company outright. Each time, he rejected the offer more or less promptly. He wasn't interested in giving up his microbrewery, nor was he interested in simply making money.

"I'd heard from others what it's like to bring in a private equity fund," says Bjergsø. "Suddenly, there are dudes in suits sitting at the end of the table making all the decisions. I just wasn't going to do that—it would be too crazy."

One day in New York, Bjergsø was introduced to Jesse Du Bey, Founder and Managing Partner of Orkila Capital. It happened somewhat circuitously. Jacob Alsing's wife was good friends with Aaron Dessner's Danish wife. Dessner, a songwriter and producer, is part of the American band The National—and he was good friends with Jesse Du Bey. One day Dessner suggested that Du Bey should look at the Danish brewery Mikkeller, because in his view something exciting was happening there.

After Bjergsø and the American private equity fund owner met for the first time, they continued talking sporadically—and the latter showed increasing interest. By that time, Mikkeller had started to become a large enterprise. The company had opened its first bars abroad and, along with the De Proef Brewery,

For a time, Mikkeller had a brewpub at the baseball stadium Citi Field, in Queens, New York, home of the New York Mets.

was producing new and innovative beers at an extraordinary rate (as many as 123 new beers in 2015 alone). The number of employees at Mikkeller's head office in Vesterbro was also growing steadily.

Despite the momentum, Bjergsø had to admit that taking the next big steps would require other resources. At the same time, having full ownership in the company had gradually become too stressful. It wasn't because he needed the money—the company was doing well and experiencing incredible growth—but he had no idea if it would last. If everything started to fall apart, having full financial responsibility could become rather costly. Although he'd considered the possibility of acquiring a partner, he never thought it would be an American private equity fund. Once he got to know Jesse Du Bey, however, the idea started to appear on his radar. The American was accustomed to investing in creative ventures and, moreover, had prominent American cultural personalities among his clients.

"It was a small private equity fund," explains Bjergsø. "He was just like the rest of us. He wore the same clothes, talked the same way, and had the same interests in music, running, and stuff like that. We became good friends. A lot of different people had applied, but I wasn't interested in just finding a partner for the money, without knowing its effect on the company. Therefore, it was important to me that, first and foremost, it was someone I could relate to on a personal level."

In 2016, Orkila Capital, with Jesse Du Bey at the helm, invested in Mikkeller and assumed a little under twenty percent of ownership. More importantly, the investment would give Mikkeller greater strength to gain a foothold in the United States and capture even more of the market around the world.

From the beginning, Bjergsø wanted growth in the company to be organic—that is, money had to be earned before investing in new ideas. He wasn't a fan of entrepreneurs who made money in one place and then spent it in another. With Orkila Capital behind it, however, Mikkeller suddenly had completely different money for investment. Expectations were also entirely different: Orkila Capital wanted something for its money, naturally, but part of the agreement was that Bjergsø still had almost complete freedom to pursue the projects he wanted to and to open bars in any location.

At that time, Bjergsø was quite interested in so-called core beers, which were intended for supermarkets, for example, to appeal to people other than wealthy big city dwellers used to frequenting bars and restaurants. To a certain extent, Mikkeller managed to change perceptions about beer in Copenhagen, but there was still plenty to do in both Europe and the rest of the world.

After being solely a nomadic brewer for so many years, Mikkeller finally acquired its own breweries. In San Diego, for example, it took over a brewery once owned by AleSmith. Bjergsø was tired of his hop beers aging too much by the time he exported them to the US. Even he didn't want to drink them, because they weren't as fresh as all the other good beers people could get there.

"There was plenty of very good, locally produced beer—and then we're sending over something from Denmark that's not only less fresh but also wildly expensive because of shipping. It just didn't make any sense. I'd rather be able to produce it over there," he says.

Within a few years, Mikkeller opened two more bars in Denmark: the brewpub WarPigs, in the Meatpacking District in Copenhagen (in collaboration with the American company 3 Floyds Brewing, making it possible to serve beer as fresh as possible), and Mikkeller Baghaven, on the industrial island Refshaleøen, where they made spontaneously fermented sour beer at their own site. From the latter bar's location on the waterfront, guests enjoyed unobstructed views of the

Baghaven in Copenhagen's hip district Refshaleøen and WarPigs in the Meatpacking District.

city center, Amalienborg Castle, and the Little Mermaid, while downing beers in the hot summer months.

Bjergsø was especially busy getting things started in Asia, where the market for microbreweries was nowhere on a par with that in the US and Europe. Mikkeller opened a number of bars on the continent—Bjergsø even dreamed of opening one in every capital in Southeast Asia. Although that proved unsuccessful, he managed to come pretty close, placing bars in Bangkok, Tokyo, Taipei, Singapore, and Seoul. For a while, South Korea was the best-selling country of all, due mainly to the fact that Mikkeller managed to brand the beer Taedonggang, named after the river that runs through neighboring North Korea's

Mikkeller's former brewpub at Citi Field in New York—designed by design studio Femmes Régionales.

capital, Pyongyang. That beer alone accounted for a third of their business.

Serious plans were also on the drawing board to open bars in both Cambodia and Laos, though they never panned out. For Mikkel Bjergsø, that was a very personal project. After he got to know Pernille Pang, who is half-Chinese, they traveled often to that part of the world. Since then, Southeast Asia has come to hold special meaning for him.

"It's clearly the continent I like best," he says, "maybe because I haven't traveled as much elsewhere. It would quickly become a problem if I also fell for Africa and South America, though—where would I go next?"

Because Mikkeller was constantly planting its flag in different places on the planet—places with vastly different cultures—holding on to the company's basic identity became increasingly important. They adhered to the tradition of placing bars in atypical locations: on side streets, in back alleys, and in murky neighborhoods. In Barcelona, for example, they didn't choose the obvious solution by finding sites on busy La Rambla, but opened instead in the old part of the Eixample district, tucked away from the largest tourist hordes. In Tokyo, they opened in the Shibuya area close to the famous traffic light for the cult film *Lost in Translation*, at Shibuya Station, the largest station in the entire capital. The bar found its home in an old garage on one of the small, hidden side streets known for sex shops and questionable bars, which only the locals know. Across the street was one of the infamous Japanese "love hotels," Hyakkendana.

"It's a slightly shady area with prostitution and love hotels. The Japanese thought it was really strange to put a bar there, but it's a cool location," says Bjergsø.

At the same time, the bar on Viktoriagade—with its light green floors, wood detailing, and whitewashed walls—served as a blueprint for all the new bars. Bjergsø wanted that underlying Scandinavian simplicity to be part of all their designs, along with certain special features that recurred, including taps on the back wall and blackboards with beer selections. Still, they didn't want to be like Hard Rock Café, which had achieved global success with its completely unified look all over the world. Instead, Mikkeller wanted to play with variations in decor, staff, uniform, food, and drinks, while maintaining a few distinctive commonalities that would become a signature uniting all of them.

"It was important that all the bars had a local feel," insists Bjergsø. "They should never be like just another bar you'd find in Vesterbro. If you open that kind of a bar in Asia, only expats will show up—and that's not why we were creating bars. They were meant for locals."

Before Mikkeller opened in Japan, for example, they had to take various cultural considerations into account. Therefore, it came in handy that the American bar manager, Hamilton Shields, had lived in Tokyo for years and had in-depth geographical and cultural knowledge about the city. Opening in these locales is nearly impossible if you don't know the language—especially if you're interested in opening a bar locals will come to for a beer after work.

In addition to the specific location serving as a draw, Mikkeller hired Japanese bartenders who didn't have English as their main language, and he tried to design the bar in a specifically Japanese style. It helped that Hamilton Shields, who had a good relationship with the local temple across from the bar, also managed to become good friends with some of the families who unofficially controlled Shibuya (which is often the case in Japanese neighborhoods).

"If he'd been a loud-mouthed American, we'd attract other types of people. But he has a very Japanese way of doing things—a Japanese mindset—and he's very humble, as one should be. That's had a huge impact on the clientele we've attracted. By comparison,

Before the opening of Mikkeller's Baghaven in the Refshaleøen district in Copenhagen.

Mikkeller has three bars in the Japanese capital of Tokyo. Left and top right: the bar in the Shibuya neighborhood. Bottom right: the burger-bar in the Kanda neighborhood.

Mikkeller's bar in Shibuya in Tokyo.

BrewDog has a bar in an area of Tokyo many expats frequent. They don't go to Shibuya that often, especially not in those small side streets, so we've attracted more locals."

Mikkeller was on a roll. The company was brewing about 50,000 hectoliters of beer every year. The selection of beers had reached more than a thousand—making Mikkeller Denmark's most successful microbrewery, with exports to around fifty countries. The largest markets were Sweden, South Korea, Great Britain, and the US. More people were hired, and Mikkeller opened bars all over the world, from Warsaw to New York, from Tórshavn to Tokyo. They had never stood still, but now Bjergsø's company was experiencing serious growth. By 2017, a company that a few years earlier had consisted of only a single bar and a handful of employees now had 400 employees in 32 bars and restaurants.

"It was completely nuts," says Bjergsø. "It was a time of much work and a lot of trips, but it was also fun. When you've created something, it's a good feeling watching it grow and get out into the world."

Anything was possible—and now Mikkeller wanted to have its own festival. The idea had barely been aired before Jacob Alsing took Aaron Dessner out to Refshaleøen, where there was a large, unused lawn at the time. It didn't take much persuasion before both the entrepreneurial musician from The National and the investor Jesse Du Bey were on board. Both had experiences with festivals: Dessner had been involved in the indie musician Bon Iver's festival, Eaux Claires, in Wisconsin, and Du Bey was the owner of the Boston festival Boston Calling.

The concept was clear: a classic music festival, but with better food and even better beer. Mikkeller would handle the drinks, and Aaron Dessner was going to draw on his various connections in the industry and curate a music program. The only thing missing was

someone to facilitate the culinary experience. They soon realized, however, whom to ask. The American lead singer and his Danish wife had lived for a while in a villa in Frederiksberg, which they rented from celebrity chef Claus Meyer while the latter was on a long business venture in New York. Therefore, Bjergsø drove up to Meyer's holiday home in North Zealand and presented him with the idea—and he wasn't hard to convince, either.

Ultimately, they reached an agreement with promoter Down the Drain, who was responsible for festivals such as the music festival NorthSide in Aarhus and would handle logistics. Everything fell into place surprisingly easily. Now, it was just a matter of setting up the festival in the middle of Copenhagen.

"For years, I had wondered why both Aarhus and Odense had a festival in the middle of the city—but not Copenhagen," says Bjergsø. "Of course, there was Distortion, but that was more of a street party. I thought Copenhagen lacked a real festival of its own."

Several of Bjergsø and Jacob Alsing's friends at Carlsberg warned them repeatedly that the project was impossible. They couldn't possibly pull such an event together in such short time. Yet, about a year later, in the summer of 2017, HAVEN Festival opened its doors with big names like Bon Iver, Band of Horses, and Iggy Pop on the poster. Naturally, Aaron Dessner's own band, The National, was the headliner. They sold 17,000 tickets—quite a number for a first-time festival, one that by and large exceeded all expectations.

Of course, the festival had its challenges, among them long queues for both the food and the toilets. Also, the bridge built to connect the two larger areas comprising the festival was too narrow; people had to constantly squeeze through a crowd to get from one place to the other. The part Mikkeller was responsible for ran pretty smoothly, even if Jacob Alsing had to make some hectic saves at the last minute. For example, after

the first day of the festival, he awoke suddenly at 4 a.m. in a state of shock in a hotel in the middle of Copenhagen. Some numbers that didn't add up suddenly appeared in his subconscious, and he sat up with an unpleasant realization: "We're going to run out of lagers."

Mikkeller had brewed equal amounts of Pale Ale and Pilsner, but festival guests had clearly thirsted after the latter. Therefore, Jacob Alsing immediately started calling other breweries to buy lagers for the second day. Early the next morning, three trucks from Amager Brewery, among others, drove into the square, and before the clock struck noon, tankers in all of the bars had been adjusted to meet the demand.

"I think Carlsberg has a hundred men working full-time at Roskilde Festival. There

Mikkel Bjergsø at the legendary Tokyo intersection made famous in the film *Lost in Translation*. Mikkeller's bar in Shibuya is not too far away.

were maybe five of us—but we succeeded anyway. That's a good indication of who we are. If we think something's cool, then we just do it. We try to see opportunities rather than limitations. Problems might arise, but then you have to fix them. I think our strength is that we've always taken the approach that if we just work harder, we'll probably succeed," says Bjergsø.

The following year, selling tickets became significantly more challenging. Down the Drain had warned Bjergsø and the others about this phenomenon in advance. The promoter said that the first year's festival would prompt new interest, but it would drop off in the second— and that turned out to be true. At the same time, other circumstances made the festival less attractive. Because there had been a

number of complaints the first year, they had to shut down at midnight every night. The vast majority of complaints had come from the restaurants at Seaside Toldboden across the water. If the wind blew in a certain direction, the music from the festival overwhelmed them.

"People are always complaining in Copenhagen. Even if there's only noise for two days. But that's just the way it is," says Bjergsø.

Creating an equally star-studded program also became a problem. Admittedly, they managed to get the German krautrock band Kraftwerk as the second festival's headliner, but Dessner had used most of his connections the first year and just couldn't repeat that lineup.

The weather was also not something to write home about, as it was one of the

hottest summers ever in Denmark. The sun had been shining for four months in a row, with temperatures above 25 degrees Celsius (77 degrees Fahrenheit). The night before the festival, there was a torrential rainstorm over Copenhagen. It woke up Bjergsø when the sky suddenly opened in a deluge. The festival stages were by no means built for such large amounts of water, making the whole thing far more chaotic than they had anticipated. Subsequently, the various parties agreed to put an end to it after two festivals.

All those problems were still in the future, however, when The National capped off the first year's festival on a Saturday night in front of a sea of people. Mikkel Bjergsø and Jacob Alsing stood watching from a distance. Both men had goosebumps:

"It was wild standing there, being part of it all, and trying to take in that you'd helped to get it all up and running. It was the greatest thing we'd ever done."

Left: Haven Festival. The sign is made with empty beer cans from Mikkeller.

Right: brothers Aaron and Bryce Dessner from the band The National, Mikkel Bjergsø, and chef Claus Meyer.

Mikkeller bars around the world. From top left: Paris. Shanghai. Little Italy in San Diego. Berlin. Oslo.

Bars and eateries from Mikkeller.
From top left: Copenhagen Airport.
La Neta in Nørrebro, Copenhagen.
Henry & Sally's in Oslo. Aarsdale
on Bornholm. Berlin. Hyggestund
in Copenhagen.

X

RICK ASTLEY'S RED LAGER

It's an early November day in 2021, and the autumn sun is casting golden rays across the Danish roads. Mikkel Bjergsø is on his way to the seaside town of Tisvilde, in North Zealand, to check out Mikkeller's latest project, a restaurant called VesterVilde. He plans to open it in collaboration with Kamilla Kristensen and Thomas Wetle Andersen, who already run the restaurant VesterØL on the island of Læsø. In recent years, VesterØl has become extremely popular and is now one of the most difficult places to get a table in all of Denmark.

Ever since it opened, VesterØL has had Mikkeller's beer on the menu, so collaborating seemed only natural. Initially, they started MikkØLler on Læsø. The bar and food truck, serving fresh beer and tasty dishes on the sunny terrace in front of the restaurant, was Bjergsø and the two restaurateurs' attempt to create a framework for a relaxed holiday atmosphere, with cold beer always at hand. Now they were considering taking a step further by opening the restaurant VesterVilde. For over ten years, Bjergsø and Pernille Pang have had a holiday home nearby—more precisely in Vejby about five kilometers away—so they've spent a lot of time in the area. By this time, Tisvilde had established itself as one of the country's major hotspots.

For several years, Bjergsø has been thinking of opening something here because, on one hand, the place attracts a lot of vacationers and on the other, according to him, it needs a serious boost in quality.

A little later in the morning, he drives past the small rowhouses along the main street and then continues into town, past a small grocery store and coffee shops. Eventually, he parks the car in front of the unfinished restaurant, not too far from the water, where artisans are in full swing.

"Okay, now we're in Tisvilde. It's a really cool location—one of the best in town."

In his early homebrewing days, Mikkel Bjergsø contacted the American microbreweries 3 Floyds Brewing and AleSmith—and to his great surprise was invited to visit both of them. He had only one thought when he flew to the US a few weeks later: "It would be fucking cool to come over and brew with them."

At that time collaborations were still a rarity in the industry; in fact, by 2007 only two famous beers had been made that way anywhere in the world. Therefore, Mikkeller's collaboration that same year with two San Diego breweries, AleSmith and Stone, was only the third time that had happened.

"Back then, breweries in San Diego might be able to help each other with hops, for example, or something like that, but collabs simply didn't exist," observes Bjergsø. "Surprisingly enough, people were extremely open and receptive to the idea. I had really wondered about that, but 3 Floyds not only let me in—they even showed me how their equipment worked."

It worked to Bjergsø's advantage that the American brewers initially found him a bit exotic because of his Danish background. At 3 Floyds Brewing, the brewers were very taken by Scandinavia and ancient Viking culture. *Pusher* was actually owner Nick Floyd's favorite movie.

"They found it funny that a Viking had come over. Also, because there was so much talk about Mikkeller in beer circles, they'd heard about it before. Otherwise, they probably wouldn't have said yes," he says.

For Mikkel Bjergsø, collaborating with two of the most prominent microbreweries in the industry at that time kickstarted an approach that would result in many unusual experiences. From Mikkeller's inception, he has tried to live up to the motto that the worst that can happen is that you hear "no." Conversely, trying could result in a new and fruitful collaboration, one that could help him to develop as a person and Mikkeller to develop as a brand. He was convinced, therefore, that he could learn from other breweries molded by completely different ideas and cultures than his own. For several years afterwards, he turned quite consistently to brewers he admired to suggest collaborations.

"I saw it as an opportunity for us to learn from each other," says Bjergsø. "Today, that goal has been somewhat lost in the numerous collabs where it's all about just doing it. I think there *has* to be an objective. It might be to learn something from it or to create something together that you wouldn't have created otherwise."

In the beginning, Bjergsø was one of the pioneers when it came to reaching out to people. At the same time, however, as collaborating became more and more widespread in the industry, he found it increasingly boring to travel around "pouring ingredients into a pot and having your picture taken." Instead, he wanted to collaborate with people with entirely different backgrounds and completely different ways of thinking—people who had absolutely nothing to do with the microbrewery scene, such as coffee roasters and farmers. All sorts of other people provided insight into new worlds that he could draw experience from and then utilize in beer brewing—from fashion designer Henrik Vibskov and knitwear interior designers LuckyBoySunday to a Danish funeral shop and various metal bands.

Among others, he entered into a collaboration with noise rock band Ring Them Bells in connection with the band's debut album in 2013. For example, Bjergsø brewed a 10 percent porter, and as the beer got hotter, the flavors stood out more distinctly. Subsequently, the beer's recipe was engraved by American artist Half-handed Cloud on the B-side of the vinyl based on the motto that rock music and beer go hand in hand.

Bjergsø was fascinated by entering into collaborations that ranged from the extremely masculine to the totally feminine yet still worked within Mikkeller's brand. As long as the microbrewery maintained a clear visual expression, he felt they could expand their universe and, as a bonus, tap into other potential fan bases. At the same time, he considered the traditional brewing industry to be conservative; these atypical collaborations were the antidote that could stimulate him on a more personal level.

"I was starting to collaborate in the beer industry, because I think it's cool to go out and work with people and learn something. If things just stay the same, I get restless fairly quickly. I think it's boring as hell to get up and do the same thing two days in a row."

While Mikkel Bjergsø was at the forefront of the burgeoning microbrewery revolution at the end of the aughts, equally revolutionary accomplishments were happening on the Danish food scene. With Copenhagen restaurant Noma at the forefront, New Nordic Cuisine, with its focus on locally sourced ingredients, became the latest trend. In its own way, Mikkeller fits perfectly into these developments. Some in the media even referred to the Danish microbrewery as "beer's answer to Noma."

Although the comparison didn't make that much sense to Bjergsø, he wasn't blind to the fact that it was good for Mikkeller's image—and that it opened doors to the gastronomic world.

"I really wanted to work with people who knew a lot about taste and processes yet did things differently than brewers. Brewing beer and cooking are two very different things. One takes at least a month, and the other you can sometimes do in three minutes," he comments.

In 2009, Bjergsø was co-organizer of a contest between beer and wine, held at Michelin restaurant Kiin Kiin in Copenhagen's hip Nørrebro neighborhood, to answer the question: Which drink is better suited to food? The competition took place over two evenings and ended in a draw—a more than honorable result, thought Bjergsø, because at that time beer didn't have the same reputation as wine.

In his eyes, something fundamentally strange was going on in the restaurant world, and it became his secret mission to change that.

"If you went to a high-end restaurant—a three-star Michelin restaurant—you knew they were spending a lot of time on the food and that they had a huge wine cellar with the best wines in the world," observes Bjergsø. "On the other hand, they'd serve crappy beer. To me, it was strange that they didn't care about that aspect. Beer actually has much greater potential than wine when it comes to pairing it with food. In beer, you can use all ingredients, while in wine you can only use one. I wanted to change all that by focusing on beers with different flavor nuances."

Bjergsø knew full well why that attitude existed. There were some obvious reasons why beer had that reputation. First, there was no training in beer similar to becoming a sommelier in the world of wine. Second, many people simply assume that beer in the supermarket shouldn't cost much more than 15 kroner (about $2.50), while wines can easily cost up to 500 kroner (about $70).

"Because beer has to be so inexpensive, restaurants obviously can't make money on it. They'd rather sell a wine for 2,000 kroner. Only in the last twenty years have people started getting into beer at home, whereas it used to be something they'd gulp down sitting on a bench. Historically, it's also more of an industrial product, while wine is an agricultural product. There are plenty of stories about the winemaker's daughter trampling on the grapes—but what can you say about beer? It's just not as exotic to say it's made in steel tanks down in a Danish suburb," comments Bjergsø.

Following the competition at Kiin Kiin, Bjergsø started crafting beer for the Thai Michelin restaurant—but it also opened the door to working with other acclaimed restaurants, such as Mission Chinese Food in San Francisco, the three-star Alinea in Chicago, and El Celler de Can Roca in Catalonia, Spain (number one on the list of the best restaurants in the world for several years). In 2011, Mikkeller also brewed a beer for Noma called Noma Novel, a type of Belgian ale created in collaboration among Bjergsø, Noma's sommelier, and owner René Redzepi. The beer, not available elsewhere, had been specially designed so that it didn't overpower the pure and delicate taste impressions in the food.

His new collaborations with various chefs meant that Bjergsø learned a great deal about differing approaches to technique, ways to combine taste and texture and ways to use ingredients to create more harmonious tastes than what people typically tried to achieve with beer. Still, several times over the years, he challenged restaurants to turn their conventional thinking upside down. For example, in 2014, he collaborated with well-known Copenhagen chef Jakob Mielcke, from Mielcke & Hurtigkarl, to launch a series of beers called MAD in which each type of beer complimented one of the five basic flavors: sweet, salty, bitter, sour, and umami.

Within this wild project, they flew forty kilos of Icelandic seaweed to the De Proef Brewery in Belgium to make an umami pilsner that would capture the ocean's fresh and salty tones. For their sweet beer, they used popcorn because of its rich taste, for the salted beer they used Japanese umeshu plums, and for the sour beer they employed the aromatic citrus fruit Yuzu in a spontaneously fermented ale. When Jakob Mielcke presented the five beers to guests at his restaurant in Frederiksberg Have, he announced that this beer wasn't crafted to be drunk while watching a soccer match. On this day, for example, the sour beer, which had a cloudy orange color, was served with king crab, pink grape jelly, and sheep cream infused with jasmine.

"Mielcke knew a lot about ingredients and temperatures that I could use in my beer brewing," explains Bjergsø. "Among other things, I learned how to extract as much

aroma as possible from specific ingredients. On the other hand, during those years I also taught these chefs something about beer—because in my view they didn't have a clue. They just weren't taking it seriously. Still, I think Noma is able to open a sister restaurant in Copenhagen today, with a focus on beer, because in all modesty I helped to make an impression on that world."

After spending a long time absorbing inspiration from the culinary world, Bjergsø found the courage to start his own restaurant in 2014. His goal was to open an open-faced sandwich spot in Copenhagen, one that in addition to its own microbrewery would offer the city's best selection of aquavit. It was a resounding success when Mikkeller opened the doors to Øl & Brød on Viktoriagade in Vesterbro, right next to the first Mikkeller bar.

Mikkeller's Øl & Brød, formerly located on Viktoriagade in Copenhagen.

Along with Swedish chef Magnus
Pettersson, Mikkeller runs Selma,
an open-faced sandwich restaurant,
in Copenhagen.

Øl & Brød was Bjergsø's contribution to combining beer and food in an appropriate way. He lured Patrick Bach Andersen and Emil Skovsgaard Bjerg as head chefs. The then twenty-one-year-old bearded and tattooed chefs had previously worked at the Michelin-starred restaurant Søllerød Kro in Holte, north of Copenhagen, where they'd won silver at the Danish open-faced sandwich championships. After their first conversation about the concept with Bjergsø, they were convinced— and three days later they started working. The restaurant offered eleven different kinds of open-faced sandwiches, each paired with its own specialty beer; the restaurant also had the country's largest selection of aquavit, with as many as five hundred from around the world.

A few years later, Øl & Brød had to close because of weak sales, but that didn't mean a final farewell to the sandwich scene. One day, Bjergsø was eating at Selma in Tove Ditlevsen's Gallery when he started conversing with head chef Magnus Pettersson, who was Swedish. The two already knew each other somewhat, and the Swede mentioned that he had to move and was looking for a new partner.

Bjergsø seized the opportunity: "Well, then I want to be your new partner."

After they opened on Rømersgade, near the Botanical Gardens, Søren Frank, the famous food critic for the Danish newspaper *Berlingske*, gave six stars to an open-faced sandwich restaurant for the first time. Frank described Selma as "more of a hipster beer bar in Vesterbro than a classic lunch hole." Selma has also won a Bib Gourmand Award, issued by the Michelin guide for "creating fantastic food at a decent price," and when *Time Out* recently posted an overview of the best eateries in Copenhagen, only Noma surpassed Selma.

In 2020, Mikkeller also started collaborating with the pizza restaurant Beberè in the northern Italian city of Milan. The restaurant, which has won the prestigious Tre Spicchi award several times for the quality of its food, is run by brothers Matteo and Salvatore Aloe. Matteo had previously worked at Noma in Copenhagen. Once he tried Mikkeller beer for the first time, he decided that he wanted the same beer in his pizza restaurant. This subsequently led to a collaboration, which now means that there is a Mikkeller bar inside the restaurant.

When Mikkel Bjergsø steps out again onto the main street in Tisvilde, clouds are rolling in and the bushes are rustling in the cool autumn wind. After spending an hour and a half with Kamilla Kristensen, Thomas Wetle Andersen, and the building managers at the as yet unfinished restaurant, he's in good spirits.

"It's going to be really good," he says. "Now we just have to open."

During the summer of 2021, Bjergsø and the two restaurateurs from VesterØL open a pop-up bottle shop featuring draft beer for takeout on the terrace in front of the upcoming restaurant. It's late July—high season for vacationers in northern Zealand—so the atmosphere is quite festive.

A few days later, he has a meeting with a traditional Danish glass designer about a possible new series of beer glasses. At this time, he's also entered into a new collaboration with the Danish fashion and lifestyle brand Wood Wood. In addition, he's in talks with lighting company Louis Poulsen to make a beer celebrating the fiftieth anniversary of the Pantella lamp, designed by his great hero, the late Verner Panton.

All things considered, plenty of potential collaboration opportunities have occurred— and new inquiries are constantly coming in. After several years of Bjergsø consistently pushing for more collaborations, the balance started to tip at some point. Now, Mikkeller is the one constantly being approached with inquiries about new partnerships.

Since then, the art has been in saying yes to the right opportunities. In some cases, that hasn't required any major decision-making, as when world-renowned film director David Lynch contacted Mikkeller about making Twin Peaks beers. In general, however, Bjergsø uses the very simple rule of thumb that if the brand is cool and the people are cool, he says yes.

"But for the most part, the people who approach us *are* cool. They usually know in advance if their own brand fits into Mikkeller's universe. Rarely do we think, 'What are you talking about?' In most cases, they're reasonably realistic. I wouldn't approach others with all sorts of crazy queries—and fortunately the same goes for most people. Sometimes you discover along the way whether the brand is any good or not. Not everything works in terms of branding," he observes.

Some years ago, Mikkeller entered into a collaboration with the organization Girls Are Awesome, which works to advance female representation in cultural life. In that regard, two "Fem" Ale beers were crafted to focus on and celebrate women in culture: a light beer called Blonde and a dark beer called Brunette. At the time, they didn't attract much attention—but in 2021, they were suddenly in the spotlight again in the wake of the MeToo movement. The beers were criticized for being stereotypical and derogatory. Although the intent was actually the exact opposite, branding hadn't been given enough consideration.

At other times, Mikkeller needed to be completely clear in advance about why they'd entered into a specific collaboration. That was the case, for example, when at one point they crafted a beer for Burger King's restaurants.

"I thought it was super-cool, because it was a way to reach a wider audience," comments Bjergsø, "but it became clear that communication was especially important in this case. Basically, people think it's weird for us to be doing something with Burger King, because it's fast food, which they associate with poor quality. But for us, it was a way to

"What can you say about beer? It's not particularly exotic to say it's made in steel tanks down in a Danish suburb."

– Mikkel Bjergsø

For years, Mikkel Bjergsø frequented the restaurant Mission Chinese Food in San Francisco. He was particularly enthusiastic about its informal atmosphere. In 2019, Mikkeller opened Vesterbro Chinese Food, which appears in the photo. However, they had to close the restaurant during the pandemic.

reach customers we never would. We don't make beer only for the elite—we make beer for everyone. If it can help provide new experiences for people that they wouldn't otherwise have, that's cool too. Once we communicated this clearly, the criticism ended."

To this day, meeting with brewers, chefs, coffee roasters, chocolatiers, and musicians—or whoever—inspires Mikkel Bjergsø the most. His mantra has always been to network without necessarily having a clear business purpose. Ever since Mikkeller established itself internationally, he's had new opportunities to travel to places he'd never imagined and to have experiences only few are granted. Among them, he has guest-brewed at microbreweries in countries as diverse as Russia, China, and Brazil. A few years ago, he was in North Korea, where he and several others from Mikkeller Running Club were allowed to participate in a race in the otherwise hermetically sealed dictatorship. While there, he established contact with a North Korean brewery, whom he invited to the subsequent Mikkeller Beer Celebration in Copenhagen. Despite taking a lot of persuasion, he finally succeeded—and it became the first North Korean brewery ever to participate in a festival outside their homeland.

Bjergsø had also dreamed of becoming the first foreign brewer in that country. He had difficulty making friends with the right people, however, and in the end it didn't pan out. On the other hand, in 2018, he became the first foreign brewer to brew beer in Bhutan. There are only four breweries in the small Buddhist kingdom in the Himalayas, and the microbrewery market is, to say the least, nothing to cheer about. Still, Bjergsø was able to visit one brewery and at the same time brew a beer for them from a recipe he had prepared. It was a so-called Sour Gose, which he made from the small, local pineapples and Himalayan salt.

Ironically, people in Bhutan are not allowed to extract salt from the very mountains where they live, as the country is extremely environmentally conscious and the only one in the world that's CO2-negative. They measure their gross domestic product in happiness, so Mikkel Bjergsø had to bring the salt he needed.

"It's pretty funny to be taking Himalayan salt with you to the Himalayas. But it actually tasted really good. It's the best damn beer brewed in that country," he says.

The idea of brewing in the small kingdom first arose because Bjergsø's partners at Mikkeller's bar in Bangkok had strong contacts in Bhutan. From there it was easy to turn ideas into actions. One of only very few people a year, he managed to enter on a work visa, which also meant he had to run around by himself without any guide.

"Bhutan is a wild country," says Bjergsø, "like going back in time a hundred years. It's not developed at all—they're still riding in horse-drawn carriages. Yet they seem to be doing well. I'd really like to go back there. It's absolutely beautiful."

Workers at the microbrewery he visited had problems carbonating their beer. They didn't think it was working properly, because once bottled, the beer turned out flat. Because Bhutan is at an altitude of 2,400 meters, Bjergsø realized he had to adapt his recipes. He asked them: "Have you taken into account that there's different air pressure up here?" They hadn't.

"I suggested that they try carbonating a little harder. And it worked. Now all their beers are better, because they're calibrated for an altitude of 2,400 meters," he explains.

Although Mikkeller has become a large and professional company, especially since 2016, Bjergsø still feels the need to make room for projects that are purely pleasurable. For example, he heard a rumor a few years back that singer Rick Astley was living on Amager in Copenhagen. He couldn't believe it—as a teenager, he had idolized the British pop star, best known for the 1980s' hit "Never Gonna Give You Up." Bjergsø heard Astley's songs repeatedly on his Walkman and had posters of him hanging on his walls. Therefore, he immediately got the idea that he had to make contact, so they could brew a beer together.

Bjergsø arranged for a case of blended Mikkeller beer to be sent to the home Astley shares with his Danish wife, Lene Bausager. As it turned out, they weren't living on Amager—they lived in London. Still, the idea had been planted, so they had to redirect the gift to the singer's home in Richmond, just outside of the capital.

When the British pop star popped open the first beers, he wasn't exactly enthused. He was used to drinking pints at the local pub, and this was a somewhat different experience—and not necessarily a better one. As he made his way through the case, however, he gradually realized that this was a beer to be enjoyed in a totally different way than he was used to.

In addition to the package from Mikkeller, Bjergsø had included an invitation for them to brew a beer together. Rick Astley agreed, and in 2017 the two men traveled together to Belgium. First, they made their way to the brewery 3 Fonteinen's restaurant on the outskirts of Brussels to eat mussels steamed in the spontaneously fermented beer Oude Geuze. While there, they also had Faro, a lambic beer made with brown sugar, and according to Rick Astley's own statement, he started to see the light.

On the other hand, Astley couldn't help but wince when Bjergsø convinced him to taste hop extract (it's a kind of initiation ritual in the brewing world to ingest the sticky, swampy green mass). Afterwards, they reached the small Belgian town of Lochristi, more specifically the De Proef Brewery, where together with master brewer Dirk Naudts they would be making a so-called red lager with a touch of ginger—a reference to both Astley's own reddish hair and to his longtime habit of always drinking honey and ginger before going on stage to perform.

A few months after their visit to the De Proef Brewery, the beer was ready to be launched on the market. The pop singer named it Astley's Northern Hop Lager, a tribute to his roots in Northern England and to the dance festivals of that time.

Originally, Bjergsø's only intent was to get permission to brew a single beer with his childhood idol, but along the way the two men developed a friendship that gave birth to new ideas. For a long time, Mikkeller had planned to open a bar in London; it seemed only natural to try to get a foothold in the capital of a country that, if anything, was known for its pub culture. Yet, that was precisely why they had to wait for just the right moment. In Rick Astley, who had lived in London for more than thirty years, Bjergsø finally found the right partner—and once he opened the British pop star's eyes to the joys of craft beer, Astley wasn't hard to convince.

Together they opened a Mikkeller Bar in the hip Shoreditch neighborhood in East London—and by the following year they opened a brewpub with twenty beers on tap and open-face sandwiches on the menu in Exmouth Market. At the pop-up's opening, Astley launched his brand-new album *Best of Me*. During his thirty-year career, he'd already sold more than forty million albums worldwide, but had taken a long break from the big stage before returning a few years earlier with his comeback album *50*.

In fact, Mikkeller's Danish design agency focused on the legendary pop musician's history when devising the concept for the brewpub The designers were inspired by the mood of one of his 80s videos, which had a unique sweetness and romance about it. Mikkeller's Art Director, Keith Shore, combined an illustration of Rick Astley with Mikkeller's visual identity into a neon sign and incorporated small details from his lyrics all around the bar.

One of Mikkel Bjergsø's strengths from early on has been his ability to master the difficult task of networking. Whenever he has

met interesting people, he hasn't hesitated to set things in motion.

"To a great extent, I've built Mikkeller's brand on collaboration," he observes, "the right breweries, the right chefs, the right musicians. Even though I'm extremely introverted, I really think I'm good at it. I'm not the type who likes to be the center of attention—and I don't like expending a lot of energy on just talking to people—but I think I'm really good at seeing the quality in what people can do and how to connect it to what I do."

To this day, Bjergsø attributes Mikkeller's success over the years to teaming up with the right people who in one way or another have contributed to some fruitful collaborations.

Famous British pop musician Rick Astley and Mikkel Bjergsø. The former is a partner in both a Mikkeller bar and a brewpub in London. At right is the brewpub in London's Exmouth district.

"One of the clearest reasons for our success is that I've always spent a lot of energy working with people who have something to offer other than beer. When I started, beer was just fucking beer—a product you took off the shelf, and basically it didn't matter which one you got hold of. I know it may sound smug, but Mikkeller has clearly redefined the way people all over the world think about beer. It has become much more of a community and a universe than simply a product, with running clubs, festivals, restaurants, and collaborations with all sorts of different people."

Left: Mikkeller's bar in Shoreditch, London.

Right: Mikkeller's brewpub in Exmouth.

XI

A HUGE PARTY

On this last Saturday in October, 2021, a large crowd of people wearing wristbands and holding small beer glasses has gathered on the cobblestones in front of Øksnehallen, an exhibition space in Copenhagen. Although a chilly autumn wind has blown in, the most dedicated have been standing here for a long time. Inside awaits beer of almost every kind—from more than eighty of the most coveted microbreweries in the world—so they can try a little of everything.

Since 2012, the annual Mikkeller Beer Celebration has been held as a two-day event featuring the best microbreweries. Although Mikkeller has also held the festival in Tokyo and Boston, the event usually takes place in Copenhagen, as it does this year.

Before long, they finally get the green light, and the herd of people race across the gray tiles and head straight for the numerous black stalls with their white and yellow signs enticing visitors with pilsner, IPAs, barley wine, lambic, and anything else found within genres of beer—even cider, one of the newest crazes. In a split second, the folding tables and benches scattered across the middle of the hall are occupied by different groups of people with loads of samples, which they taste thoroughly, jointly assessing them with the appropriate seriousness.

For a long time, it has been customary for guests at the festival to decide their taste-testing strategies in advance, so they can sample as much beer as possible. They bring extra glasses, maybe even chips and bowls, and then they send each other around in an organized fashion to experience the perfect mini-selection at each table. Over the course of the festival's weekend, they'll have the opportunity to taste about 1,000 different beers—the vast majority of them at the four main sessions, where some two hundred new beers are on tap at any given time. However, up to forty different events are also held in the days surrounding the festival, including *tap takeovers*, where a brewery takes over the blackboard at one of Mikkeller's bars one evening; *releases* in the two Mikkeller bottle shops; and *tastings* and *food pairings* in the restaurants.

It's impossible to say exactly how many beers someone can consume over the course of one weekend—but in 2016 the culture magazine *Vice* found three student friends from Skåne, Sweden who estimated that they'd have enough time to taste a total of 400 beers. Also, they had devised tactics to get enough beer brought to their communal table, which they could consume in "small sips" so they wouldn't get too drunk too fast.

Many of the attendees tick off the different beers on the app Untappd. On the weekend of 2019, that number reached a quarter of a million beers. Since far from everyone registers what they consume, the only thing that can be said with certainty is that *a lot* of beer is served. In fact, far more beers will be served over the counter during the Mikkeller Beer Celebration than at a typical beer bar that's open 365 days a year.

In 2011, after Mikkel Bjergsø had had his first Mikkeller bar on Viktoriagade for a year, he decided to hold a birthday party. He invited a lot of different brewers that he'd gotten to know in the industry to put their own beers on tap in his bar. Before he knew it, the whole event had grown into one gigantic brewer-fest.

The following year he decided to do it again. Because he had good contacts at the running club Sparta, located in the Østerbro neighborhood, he managed to rent the Sparta Hall for the weekend. That way, he'd have enough room for even more brewers—after all, they were the ones he really wanted to celebrate. He christened the event the "Copenhagen Beer Festival," squeezed in eighteen brewers, and sold a thousand tickets.

At that time, Copenhagen already had an official beer festival, but in his view there was too much focus on the quantity of beer and on people getting drunk—and not enough

Mikkeller has held the Mikkeller Beer Celebration since 2012. Top: a picture from Øksnehallen in Copenhagen, the setting for the festival since 2015.

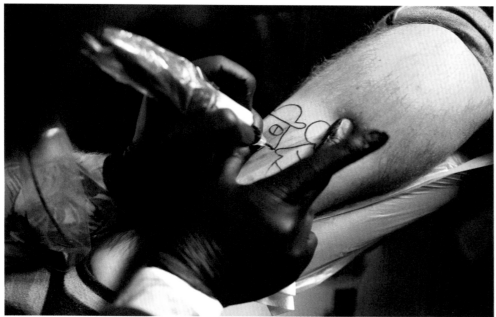

Mood shots from Mikkeller Beer Celebration. It is customary for rare bottles to be opened at the festival —which tends to attract people, evident on page 182-183. Some also get tattoos from the various breweries during the festival.

on the quality and the social aspect. Bjergsø wanted to change all that with Mikkeller's own festival.

"The beer festival in Copenhagen at the time was like a trade show," recalls Bjergsø. "The brewers were having fun together, but they had no interaction with the guests. In fact, they often found it annoying when guests came with their tickets, because then they had to interrupt their own socializing to serve them. I wanted to change all that and just throw a big party—and that's still the way it is. People show up, drink beer, and have fun."

Many of the brewers at the first official festival were Bjergsø's own friends: those who had helped teach him how to brew beer and had shared recipes with him, and those who, conversely, he had taught to brew beer and with whom he had shared recipes. Since then, the festival has continued to grow, becoming an event that beer nerds the world over mark on their calendars as the highlight of the year. Over the years, it has become a huge celebration featuring all kinds of breweries, where people meet and celebrate beer with a lot of other beer lovers.

His original intention was to create a festival for brewers and not for customers. Not because the latter were unimportant—on the contrary—but Bjergsø felt that if he made the brewers happy first, they'd be more willing to present their best beer and, ultimately, make their customers happy too.

The hungriest of the guests for this year's festival have placed themselves outside in the white tents erected by the food stalls, where they can find two of Copenhagen's trendy restaurants, Ramen to Bīiru and La Neta. They'll also see charismatic hot dog man John Michael Jensen handing loads of hot dogs over the counter at John's Hotdog Deli. Inside Øksnehallen, the breweries that have garnered the most hype this year are obvious. At some stalls, queues form in fewer than twenty minutes—as at Belgian Bofkont and Swedish

Omnipollo, two of the most iconic microbreweries. Some guests even want autographs and to have their pictures taken.

The special thing about the Mikkeller Beer Celebration—which the festival changed its name to after the first few years—is that the actual brewers from each attending brewery are the ones pouring the beer that guests can drink. From the start, Bjergsø was eager that the actual brewers, not some random envoy, should be presenting the various exciting and high-quality beers.

Typically, more than ninety percent of the brewers are foreign—the majority of them tend to be American, who've traditionally been about ten years ahead of the European market. In general, however, there's beer from all corners of the world. Mikkeller tries to ferret out cool and upcoming breweries, which they then combine beautifully with more traditional old-school breweries from, for example, Germany and Belgium. Each brewery that participates brings eight different beers, which means two per session: that way, they can change it all every so often. Some breweries come up with wildly different styles of beer, while others, such as the German breweries, often produce only one particular style.

Only about a fifth of the guests attending the Mikkeller Beer Celebration are Danish. The rest represent many different countries. The largest group are Swedes, who typically comprise about a third of the attendees, something which can be heard this afternoon. Dialects and accents from all over the world create the festival's soundtrack.

Early on, Bjergsø decided that the festival should be a cavalcade of stars featuring the world's best microbreweries—a festival people were willing to travel long distances to be a part of. Therefore, over the years he's been ultra-selective about which microbreweries were allowed to participate. As soon as one festival ends, Mikkeller starts planning

the next. They can quickly become pressed for time if they don't get off to a good start. Typically, it takes about ten months to arrange a successful festival. As a matter of principle, they rethink the entire concept every time; if they determine that some of the breweries are just there for a free ride, they replace them with new ones. Because so much happens constantly in the microbrewery industry—old breweries disappear and new ones surface—Mikkeller makes every effort to include interesting breweries that represent the industry's latest trends.

After holding the Mikkeller Beer Celebration in Sparta Hallen in Østerbro for several years, in 2015 they moved the event to the larger venue of Øksnehallen in Vesterbro. Although the festival more than doubled in size—drawing 2,500 guests for each of the

Mikkeller Beer Celebration has been held abroad on several occasions. Both Boston and Tokyo have served as settings for the festival.

The year Mikkeller Beer Celebration was held in Meiji Jingu Gaien, a park area with a stadium in Tokyo.

four four-hour sessions around which the festival is built—tickets also flew off the shelves this time.

That gave Bjergsø and Mikkeller the idea to take the festival outside Denmark's borders. Therefore, the following year, the Mikkeller Beer Celebration was held in Boston at City Hall Plaza, which for years has provided the setting for other major festivals. Holding the event on the other side of the Atlantic where the microbrewery scene was significantly larger than in Europe and where Mikkeller had a strong reputation seemed only natural. Musicians such as Yo La Tengo and Lucero played the festival. Mikkeller collaborated with the large, local event company Crash Line Productions, which, among others, is behind the popular annual Boston Calling Music Festival.

When Bjergsø and the others from Mikkeller flew into Boston prior to the event and looked down from the plane on all the tents in the town hall square in front of the FBI building, they had to pinch themselves. Even though Mikkeller was still a relatively small brewery, they had managed to arrange an event that would attract 6,000 enthusiastic people.

Since then, the festival has been held twice in Tokyo at the Meiji Jingu Gaien complex, a baseball field in the middle of the Japanese capital, and attended by about forty breweries from Asia, Europe, and the United States. In 2020, Mikkeller also held a festival focusing on wild yeast-fermented beer, which was a third in capacity and took place on Refshaleøen. The event featured about thirty breweries from countries such as Belgium, USA, and England, along with more untraditional places such as Argentina. Through the festival, Mikkel Bjergsø wanted to spread the wild yeast phenomenon, which in his view is one of the most experimental and exciting in microbrewery.

Currently, Mikkeller has numerous projects on the drawing board, including a version of the Mikkeller Beer Celebration in which participants start in Hirtshals, on Denmark's northwestern coast, and sail 36 hours to Tórshavn in the Faroe Islands. Sessions are also held on the ferry, and there's a three-day beer festival on Faroese soil. Participants then sail 36 hours back to Denmark. They're also considering festivals in Bhutan and Nepal, where half of the events would be held in each country. Initial meetings have already been held with relevant people from both countries.

For Bjergsø, it's a way to keep the festival relevant, so that brewers, customers—and he—don't become bored: "I can see in both myself and many of the customers that we need something new. I can't be bothered going to beer festivals where people just stand around talking about fucking beer."

Mikkel Bjergsø at the Mikkeller Beer Celebration in Tokyo.

191

XII

UN
COM
PROMIS
ING

After Mikkeller opened its first two foreign bars in San Francisco and Bangkok, respectively, the third followed a little closer to home—in Stockholm—and for good reasons. For many years, Sweden was actually Mikkeller's best market, and even today the neighboring country remains very high on the list.

"We've started to catch up here at home, but for many years sales were much, much better in Sweden. For a long time in Denmark, only beer nerds had heard of us, but many Swedes knew Mikkeller because we had our beer in the government-run liquor stores. It was a brand that ordinary people had a relationship with," says Bjergsø.

When the bar on Döbelnsgatan in Stockholm's vibrant Norrmalm district opened its doors in 2014, there was a queue as far as the eye could see. Yet even though business was going well there, Bjergsø was dissatisfied. They had tried to design the bar in Mikkeller style—with large decorations by Art Director Keith Shore on the walls, for example—but something seemed off. The bar never seemed to capture the right atmosphere. As a kind of litmus test, Bjergsø had always taken the approach that if he didn't want to come to a certain place, then something was wrong with either the service, the decor, the selection, or something entirely different—regardless of its popularity. This is how he felt about the new bar in Stockholm:

"Every time I went there, our partner had changed something around. Suddenly there was a television in the bathroom, for example, and there shouldn't be any television in the bathroom. It wasn't a sports bar. It was like that all the time."

Although the bar in Stockholm had tremendous sales—to this day that bar earned back its investment faster than any other—Bjergsø had no option but to close it. He and his Swedish business partner simply didn't have the same perception of quality. For some inexplicable reasons, they couldn't communicate clearly with each other; since Bjergsø wasn't interested in putting out fires at home and in Sweden, he turned the key after only nine months.

"Mikkeller was my brand," explains Bjergsø. "It should be the way I wanted it, or I might as well just open something else. It's fine to open a new beer bar, but don't call it Mikkeller if it doesn't live up to the standard. It was more important for me to have bars that represented what Mikkeller meant to me than it was to make money."

Roughly the same fate befell Mikkeller's first bar in Tokyo. Back in 2015, the bar opened in the Japanese capital at Shibuya's Center Gai, also known as "Basketball Street," where there was phenomenal interest in the experimental beers from the Danish microbrewery. More than 1,000 people showed up to stand in long queues in front of the small pub, which was jampacked. On that opening day, however, Bjergsø had already told his Norwegian partners that he would be closing the bar.

One of Bjergsø's acquaintances—Hamilton Shields, an American who had taken up residence in Japan—had originally set him up with the Norwegians, but even he could see early on that it just wasn't going as planned. Problems in the collaboration had already surfaced while the bar was still under construction. Bjergsø became convinced that they wouldn't be able to work together in the long run.

"One of the partners was somewhat of a scam artist," recalls Bjergsø, "a dreamer claiming he knew a lot of things. But when you started digging a little, he didn't know shit. Hamilton thought they were behaving like idiots. They already owned a café in Tokyo where they didn't pay their employees and treated them badly. Everything imaginable was an obstacle. He told me that I'd ruin my brand if I worked with them. So, I sent the Norwegians the message that I wanted to buy them out. They didn't like that, so I decided to just close the bar completely."

The best way to characterize Mikkel Bjergsø is that he's uncompromising and extremely detail-oriented. He has frequently rejected the idea that he's particularly creative. Although he seems like a man who never runs out of ideas, he's actually good at absorbing impressions and focusing on small details that he can then recreate in his own image. In principle, at Mikkeller it's a short hop from thought to action—if Bjergsø gets an idea he believes in, he establishes a tight deadline and gets started, instead of talking about it endlessly.

On the other hand, he can spend an eternity perfecting the final product, which has been both his weakness and his strength. When he was named Owner-Manager of the Year at PwC in Hellerup in 2017, they referred to him as a "perfectionist" with a "focus

Pernille Pang and Mikkel Bjergsø were a couple for many years and have two children together. Today they remain good friends working closely at Mikkeller.

on even the smallest details." Conversely, for years he has had difficulty relinquishing responsibility and delegating. He's fully aware that, at times, that has been a profound problem for him as Mikkeller's leader, yet he simply hasn't been able to let go. On numerous occasions, he has spent unimaginable amounts of time obsessing down to the last detail before being satisfied. When Mikkeller opened WarPigs, he spent forever picking out the perfect American diner cups—even the little pink packets of sugar had to be just right.

While others have sometimes found Bjergsø's obsession with perfection amusing, he fails to see the irony. He gets annoyed when things aren't done properly. He would view it as a personal defeat, for example, to open a ramen place that in its design might just as well be any other restaurant. On that front, Bjergsø can't do things eighty percent. That's why he was an elite runner in his youth, then stopped suddenly, took a fifteen-year break, and then returned to start running 100 kilometers a week. If he can't do his very best, he won't do it at all.

Bjergsø applies that same form of determination to his creative process. He has total confidence in his own taste, which he has always used as an unconditional guiding force in Mikkeller's development. He has stated repeatedly that he'd never invite a tasting panel in to judge a beer before releasing it. He prefers only making beer that he would drink—and only opening bars that he would want to visit.

One consequence of Bjergsø's perfectionism is that employees at Mikkeller's various bars and restaurants find it seriously annoying whenever Bjergsø and Pernille Pang show up. She's just like Bjergsø. As a child, Pang grew up with a father who was a waiter in the Chinese restaurant business. She often sat in the kitchen or restaurant waiting for him to be free while observing the daily routine in such a busy place. She also had an intuitive interest in aesthetics, design, and decor—as

a teenager she would redecorate her room every two weeks because she kept coming up with an even better design.

Whenever they'd visit any of Mikkeller's various locations, the two would immediately start writing lists of what wasn't working and then send them to that manager, who had to rectify any problems. They couldn't understand how a dead potted plant, for example, could be sitting there looking so pathetic and why someone hadn't automatically changed it. It came down to the smallest detail, even the right soap dispenser, because in their eyes going to the bathroom should also be a positive experience. They were extremely detail-oriented; even if they went to a restaurant that had nothing to do with Mikkeller, they couldn't stop themselves from evaluating the experience.

"I'm very controlling and detail-oriented," admits Bjergsø. "If I've opened a bar, I really have a problem with employees changing things in what I think is a bad way. Maybe there's a manager who's there on a daily basis and has his finger on the pulse of the place—and then I should just relinquish responsibility and accept that he knows what he's doing. But I'm just not good at that. On the other hand, I believe part of our success is that I'm so extremely detail-oriented."

For many years, Bjergsø checked everything, because deep down he felt he could have done it better. If he encountered employees at Mikkeller who weren't as ruthlessly dedicated to the brand as he was, it would annoy him. "I have a hard time when people cut corners. I readily admit that. Basically, I just don't understand it. One of the main reasons I love Japan so much is that they are seriously dedicated to whatever they do. No matter what people do, they just do it properly. Over there, I almost get an inferiority complex, because they think of everything."

For several years, Mikkeller and the famous microbrewery 3 Floyds talked about opening something together. Bjergsø had known the

American brewers since 2007, when he first traveled to the US to visit them. Since then, he and the Floyd brewers had kept in touch and become good friends. The American brewers visited Copenhagen several times, and Bjergsø visited them often as well. They also took various trips together throughout Europe, especially to traditional beer countries such as Belgium and Germany.

For Bjergsø, Nick Floyd was a huge inspiration, one of the best brewers in the industry. Floyd founded 3 Floyds Brewing in Munster near Chicago in 1996, and since then it has gained an almost legendary reputation in craft beer. For several years in a row, 3 Floyds was named the world's best brewery on RateBeer. The brewery is also behind the ultra-hyped beer event Dark Lord Day, when they sell their Russian imperial stout named Dark Lord in limited quantities, only on this one day. The company—using the branding "It's Not Normal"—had become known for its uncompromising and confrontational beers. Therefore, they were a good match for Mikkeller, who'd been pushing the envelope with its innovative beers on the other side of the Atlantic.

Over the years, the two microbreweries have collaborated on several beers, including the Goop series of barley-wines, utilizing different ingredients such as oats, rye, and wheat. In addition, 3 Floyds was a regular at the Copenhagen Beer Celebration right from its start. One year, one of the three owners, Barnaby Struve, even got a Mikkeller tattoo. In 2016, they finally opened their joint venture, WarPigs, in Copenhagen's Meatpacking District. The name actually resulted from a bit of a coincidence. The American brewers had always been fond of heavy metal and had cultivated the genre in their own expression. So, one day while tossing around ideas, someone suggested they name the bar after one of Black Sabbath's most famous hard rock songs. And that was that.

WarPigs was meant to be a brewpub in the American tradition. Bjergsø wanted

> # "I find it hard dealing with people who take the easy way out. I readily admit that. Basically, I don't understand it."
>
> – Mikkel Bjergsø

Named after a Black Sabbath song, the brewpub WarPigs in Copenhagen's Meatpacking District maintains a heavy metal aesthetic.

to create a bar that would be different from the approximately twenty-five bars and restaurants Mikkeller had opened by that time. He wanted to take a small step away from his classic designs and, instead, try to create a completely different kind of space. A 1,000-square-meter building with old slaughterhouse facilities provided just the opportunity. They set up a large number of table and bench sets, both indoors and outdoors, with room for more than two hundred guests. The bar's twenty taps were fitted with bone-shaped handles to reinforce the heavy metal aesthetic. Mikkeller could have opened five other bars with the cost of the specially designed brewery, made in Germany to accommodate 2,000-liter tanks—but it enabled them to serve beer that went directly from fermented tanks to serving tanks and then straight out of the tap. First, they analyzed the waterworks at Lake Michigan, where 3 Floyds is located, so they could purify the water at WarPigs to get the same taste.

Having the name of the American microbrewery on the building's façade immediately created hype. Suddenly Danes could get beer in Copenhagen's Meatpacking District that they couldn't get in the US—unless they were willing to travel all the way to 3 Floyds Brewing south of Chicago.

"Many people asked, 'Why are you making beer in Copenhagen when you can't even get it here?' But we were good friends, and they thought it was cool to come over here," says Bjergsø.

WarPigs wasn't just about beer, however. The bar would also be serving Texas-style barbecue, which was Mikkel Bjergsø's idea. Having traveled several different places in the south-central state, he'd discovered the dish, which started with leftover carvings butchers had no use for.

"Once you've carved out the tenderloin, what's left is basically waste," observes Bjergsø. "At some point, though, they discovered that if you put what's left in a smoker at a low temperature for a really long time, it became edible—nice and tender. So, the carvings you use are what you wouldn't normally use. That way, there's something positive about it. It's completely different than steak, where you take all the best parts and throw out the rest."

Bjergsø procured a high-quality smoker for WarPigs, so that American chef Andrew Hroza could smoke up to a ton of meat a day. They also copied the exact concept from the Texan barbecue places: all the decadent stuff is dispensed with and there are no waiters. Instead, you line up to order and then carry your food on a tray to your table.

"It's self-serve," he explains. "You stand in line to buy your food and clean up after yourself at the McDonalds-like trash bins. You might have to stand in line for an hour because there are so many people, only to get to the counter and find out that what you want is unfortunately sold out. The meat needs up to fourteen hours in a smoker, so we have to put the meat in overnight—and we don't want a lot of waste, because we have to throw out the rest. Ideally, the last guest buys the last piece of meat, but it's impossible to time that. So pretty much every day is sold out, and a few people have to go home disappointed. At first, people had a hard time grasping the concept. Many of them thought it was really strange."

On opening day in Copenhagen, people could also buy Mexican Coca-Cola, which Bjergsø had been eager to procure. Unlike the Coca-Cola produced in the US and Europe, the Mexican version is made with cane sugar and has become quite popular in Texas (which borders Mexico). So, if the place was really supposed to be "Texan" in spirit, people should be able to get it there.

Initially, he asked Carlsberg, which imports Coca-Cola in Denmark, if he could get a few pallets of it. That proved impossible,

WARPIGS

WarPigs opened in 2015 as a collaboration between Mikkeller and the American brewery 3 Floyds. Today, Mikkeller is the sole owner of the concept. In addition to beer, you can order Texas-style barbecue.

WarPigs has its home in old slaughterhouse buildings in the Meatpacking District in Copenhagen's Vesterbro neighborhood.

however, because it was too small a delivery. Therefore, he had to think outside the box. Bjergsø had his American partner buy two pallets at a Mexican supermarket in Los Angeles and then had them shipped to Copenhagen. On the day they arrived, he happened to be meeting with the same Carlsberg employee he had initially consulted. When he saw the two pallets, the man exclaimed: "Well, I'll be damned—you made it work anyway."

Mexican Coca-Cola wasn't the only distinctive feature to be found at the opening. As mentioned, Bjergsø had also acquired 30,000 small pink packets of sugar, the same kind people could get in the Southern states. When Mikkeller opened his first Ramen to Bīiru restaurant a few years later, he also procured the perfect water glasses—brown glasses in dappled plastic that he'd seen at ramen places in Tokyo and just had to have. That was easier said than done, however. One of his employees had to search a long time before finally locating them in a trade store in the US and then had them exported to Denmark.

Mikkeller opened the first small, intimate Ramen to Bīiru in the Nørrebro neighborhood with Japanese restaurateur Daisuke Uki. Mikkel Bjergsø had previously been introduced to aspects of Chinese cuisine by Pernille Pang, and afterwards it became a large part of their lives. Over time, they've consumed tons of dim sum at Fu Hao, a restaurant on Colbjørnsensgade in Vesterbro, where as a teenager Pang used to go with her father. In fact, Pang and Bjergsø have eaten there so often that they've long since memorized the entire menu.

Over the past twenty years, Bjergsø has indulged in as much Asian food as possible, always filling his refrigerator with different chili sauces from the continent. While traveling frequently in Japan a few years ago, in connection with the opening of Mikkeller's bar in Tokyo, he discovered the joys of ramen. He fell in love with the concept and, wondering why no one in Denmark had opened such an eatery, he decided he had to do it.

"When you open bars," explains Bjergsø, "at some point it all becomes routine. It's always about the same thing. 'How many taps should we have?' Stuff like that. I'd already done a lot of that, so I needed to challenge myself to create something totally new."

However, Bjergsø wasn't only interested in opening a restaurant with ramen on the menu—he wanted to open an authentic place where people felt as if they were eating ramen in Japan. Although the dish has its roots in China, the yellowish wheat noodles with eggs found their way to the Japanese port of Yokohama over a hundred years ago, where they were first served in modest chicken soups. The dish then spread, mutating into local versions, at first as a street phenomenon at soup carts. It became more widespread after World War II, when there was a shortage of food, so that today the dish is considered Japanese. Each Japanese ramen cook has his or her own unique recipe, which they've carefully nurtured for many years.

Long before the restaurant's opening in Nørrebro, Bjergsø brought ramen chef Takuro Otani to Denmark, so he could adapt to his new surroundings and prepare his dishes just as he would in Japan. Otani, who comes from Sapporo, a mecca for ramen with about 1,500 ramen bars, imported ready-made noodles from his hometown of Hokkaido; he then spent half a year getting the soup exactly as he wanted it by refining everything from the onions to the hardness of the water.

That was right in Bjergsø's wheelhouse. They even managed to recreate the payment

The first Ramen to Bīiru restaurant opened in Copenhagen's Nørrebro area in 2015. Diners there can get the Japanese noodle soup of the same name, which has gained traction in several European cities in recent years.

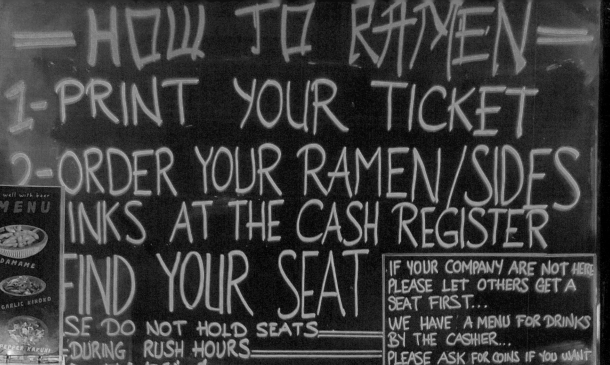

= HOW TO RAMEN =

1 - PRINT YOUR TICKET

2 - ORDER YOUR RAMEN/SIDES
INKS AT THE CASH REGISTER
FIND YOUR SEAT
SE DO NOT HOLD SEATS
- DURING RUSH HOURS

らーめんとビール

IF YOUR COMPANY ARE NOT HERE
PLEASE LET OTHERS GET A
SEAT FIRST...
WE HAVE A MENU FOR DRINKS
BY THE CASHIER...
PLEASE ASK FOR COINS IF YOU WANT
TO BUY A BEER FROM THE VENDING MACHINE

er that goes well with beer
DE MENU
EDAMAME
MED...
GARLIC KINOKO
PEPPER KAYUKI

らーめんとビール

PRINT
TICKET HERE ↓ ↓ ↓

PAY AT THE
CASHIER →

Ticket Vender

発売中   お札中止
中止   つり切れ
おつり・返却
ただいまの金額
500 100 50 10

1000

MISO   SHIO   SHOYU   MONTHLY SPECIAL

SPICY #1 MISO   SPICY #2 MISO   SPICY #3 MISO   SPICY #4 MISO

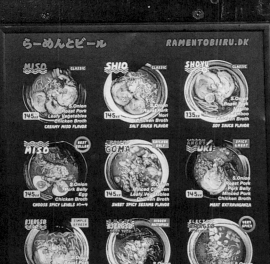

らーめんとビール   RAMENTOBIIRU.DK

MISO   CLASSIC   SHIO   CLASSIC   SHOYU   CLASSIC
                                            S.Onion
S.Onion   S.Onion   Roast Pork
Roast Pork   Roast Pork   Naruto
Nori   Nori   Bamboo
Leafy Vegetables   Chicken Broth   Chicken Broth
Chicken Broth   SALT SAUCE FLAVOR   SOY SAUCE FLAVOR
145   CREAMY MISO FLAVOR   145   135

MISO   BEST SELLER   GOMA   CHICKEN ONLY   UKI   ANGRY   SPICY MEAT
                                            S.Onion
S.Onion   S.Onion   Roast Pork
Pork Belly   Minced Chicken   Naruto
Egg   Leafy Vegetables   Minced Pork
Chicken Broth   Chicken Broth   Chicken Broth
145   CHOOSE SPICY LEVELS #1~4   145   SWEET SPICY SESAME FLAVOR   145   MEAT EXTRAVAGANZA

BJERGSØ   SIMPLE FRESH   BJERGSØ   HIDDEN MASTERPIECE   ELECTRIC ANGER   VERY SPICY
                                            S.Onion
                      S.Onion   Roast Pork
                      Pork Belly   Minced Pork
                      Nori   Tofu
145   145   145

RAMENTOBIIRU
SHIO   CLASSIC   SHOYU   CLASSIC
S.Onion   S.Onion
Roast Pork   Roast Pork
Nori   Nori
135   SALT SAUCE FLAVOR   SOY SAUCE

GOMA   UKI   ANGRY
S.Onion   S.Onion
Minced Chicken   Roast Pork
Leafy Vegetables Minced Pork
145   SWEET SPICY SESAME FLAVOR   145   MEAT EXT

BJERGSØ   HIDDEN MASTERPIECE   ELECTRIC ANGER

system by acquiring a rather kitschy Japanese ticket vending machine: you punch in your order, hand the ticket to the chefs, and then sit down at a table.

"Basically, you have no interaction at all, but in general Japan is very private. You can enter a ramen place, sit in a booth, eat, and then go out again without ever interacting with anyone else. It's the essence of that culture. I wanted to recreate that in this concept. I think it's extremely important that it feels Japanese when, for example, you open a place serving ramen. You should enter Ramen to Bīiru and feel as if you're stepping into a restaurant in Japan."

It was important to Mikkel Bjergsø that Ramen to Bīiru was as authentic as possible: it had to feel like stepping into a Japanese ramen bar. Therefore, Mikkeller acquired the same ticket system as used in Japan.

However, Bjergsø created more than his Japanese-style destination in the middle of Copenhagen. Koelschip, in Nørrebro, is his take on an authentic lambic beer bar, the kind you find in small Belgian villages. Ever since he started delving deeper into the world of beer during his younger days in Copenhagen, he has had a special love for Belgian beer. At every occasion, he's highlighted Orval as the best beer in the world and even had the brand's logo tattooed on his left upper arm. Although Mikkeller, in many ways, represents the exact opposite of traditional Belgian breweries that have refined the same few beer styles for centuries, Bjergsø has always been inspired by them—especially the lambic breweries that are constantly working to optimize even the slightest nuances.

Ironically enough, the first time he tasted spontaneously fermented lambic beer, Bjergsø found it disgusting. He could only describe the Rosé de Gambrinus, from the brewery Cantillon, as a mixture of vomit, horse stable, and vinegar. Since then, the type of beer produced using spontaneous fermentation—in which hops and wort are poured into open metal vessels and oxygenated in an environment rich in bacteria and wild yeast—has become his favorite. After traveling around Belgium for years, Bjergsø managed to amass a huge collection of lambic beers: more than 500 old, special beers and bottles, many of which were also rare. Because lambic beer is spontaneously fermented, it can last almost forever; his collection had grown to a size he couldn't possibly complete. In 2015, when Mikkeller's first bottle

In the Nørrebro neighborhood, Mikkeller has opened the bar Koelschip, Mikkel Bjergsø's take on an authentic lambic bar, like those found in Belgium. Bjergsø enjoys the special Belgian type of beer. At bottom right, the Belgian ambassador to Denmark making a speech at the opening, next to the famous beer writer Carsten Berthelsen.

Mikkeller and Ricardo Medrano Treviño are the driving forces behind the Mexican street-kitchen restaurant La Neta. They opened the first La Neta in Nørrebro in 2018.

shop moved from the smaller extra room at Mikkeller & Friends to Torvehallerne open-air market, Bjergsø turned the room into Koelschip, a Belgian-style beer bar. He relocated his entire private collection, which was only gathering dust at home, to Koelschip. Now, people can experience one of the largest collections of lambic beer in the world, with bottles dating back to the 1950s, right there in Nørrebro. Old curtains hanging at the room's entrance exude that rural Belgian warmth, and inside the space is dark, cozy, and full of nostalgic memorabilia hidden under hop vines hanging from the ceiling.

"It looks like you're in an old lambic bar in a Belgian village," says Bjergsø. "I love going to places like that in Belgium, but unfortunately people don't totally understand it. You have to be a beer nerd to get it—and there just aren't enough of them for that. Still, I think it's one of our coolest places in Copenhagen."

One time while he was in Stockholm, Bjergsø stumbled upon the Mexican street food-style restaurant La Neta. He loved Mexican food, especially tacos when they were made properly, and had always wondered why it was so hard to find high-quality examples in Copenhagen. And now he'd found it—in the Swedish capital, of all places.

"I thought it was super cool. It was like being in Mexico—it had the same vibe—so that very evening I got hold of the owner and asked if we should open one in Copenhagen. He was on board with that."

The second La Neta opened on Nørrebrogade in Copenhagen in the summer of 2018, this time in collaboration with Mikkeller. In addition to spicy food, the taqueria served both mezcal and tequila, and to be faithful to the original concept, a real tortilla press was purchased from Mexico. For the opening, Bjergsø had painstakingly obtained 40-ounce bottles of Mexican Sol: he viewed the large, almost one-and-a-half-liter bottled beer—sometimes seen being drunk out of paper bags—as synonymous with authentic Mexican street kitchens.

"It was just a gimmick, like so many other things, and maybe only a few of the customers even get the references. But for those who do, it's pretty damn cool."

XIII

FAT AND LAZY

Copenhagen's Meatpacking District is teeming with people in front of the white industrial building with blue windows. "WarPigs," in characteristic black font, appears above the entrance. Puddles of water have gathered on the black benches, and runners in every possible outfit—some in red and blue striped running suits, some in reflective gear, and others in gray and black—are scurrying around on the wet asphalt in front of the building. In the middle of the throng of young and old, men and women, Søren Runge is standing on a bench and trying to slice through the noisy crowd.

"When we get back, there'll be a beer waiting for you," he shouts to great applause from those present. A moment later they begin their preliminary warm-up around Vesterbro. It's a small route of exactly 1.6 kilometers (the equivalent of an English mile), one which all the running club's other chapters run on the same day. This particular Saturday in the beginning of October is a special one, however, as it's Mikkeller Running Club's seventh birthday, celebrated in over a hundred different cities around the world.

The running club—founded in 2014 on the philosophy that if you enjoy good beer and physical activity, you've found the perfect balance in life—has grown so large that more than 20,000 runners worldwide are now affiliated in one way or another. In their established tradition, the various running clubs meet on the first Saturday of each month with different planned routes, speeds, and distances, and then enjoy a well-deserved beer or two afterwards.

In Copenhagen, Mikkeller Running Club has about fifteen captains, each of whom plans routes and makes sure to keep to the pre-agreed-upon pace. Runners can train from Monday to Friday, and events are held every third Saturday at Mikkeller Baghaven, along with the first Saturday of the month, where for a long time up to 500 runners have participated in Copenhagen.

"We've always insisted that anyone can participate, and we try to motivate everyone to think it's fun," says Søren Runge a little later, once the noise from the crowd has died down. "Mikkel's original idea with the running club, in addition to losing weight himself, was to get those big, heavy beer drinkers to start moving a little."

Runge, the only one on the payroll, calls it a kind of event job. As the running club grew, with branches in such places as Brazil, it became necessary to have someone to take care of all the practicalities.

"While it's incredibly grassroots and you can do whatever you want," explains Runge, "there are some basic principles they have to follow. We have a simple manual that we give to the various branches, and then we feel that the rest will take care of itself."

Søren Runge pushes a couple rolling tables carrying cardboard boxes filled with Mikkeller beer onto the asphalt in front of WarPigs. Because he has been injured, he can't participate on this first Saturday in October, when the autumn chill has really taken hold of the capital.

"Naturally, it's a big day," he says, stopping at the sudden sound of rapidly approaching feet. "Are they coming back now?"

Shortly thereafter, the frontrunners with their sweaty foreheads arrive, followed by the rest in an elongated tail behind them. No one misses the chance to get their hands on a can of beer. Both the non-alcoholic wheat ale, Drink'in the Sun, in yellow cans with Keith Shore's distinctive figures, and a purple lager called Visions are available. Once the runners have quenched their thirst, Søren Runge whistles to drown out the crowd and then takes the floor again:

"Okay! Well done," he says, quickly advertising the numerous events that will take place under the auspices of Mikkeller Running Club in the following month. Runge then turns the floor over to the captains, who present the team they're responsible

for. They're usually named after the captain's favorite beer: New Black, You Fuck Me Up, Beer Geeks, etc. There's also a walking team for the few injured runners who still get to be part of the birthday celebration. After a group picture, everyone is sent away again, and the Meatpacking District is once again quiet (at least for a little while).

"In the past, we'd run around to all of Mikkeller's bars and restaurants on these birthdays, but in recent years it's become impossible. There are just too many places. People got really drunk last year—it was too much," says Søren Runge, laughing as he trudges toward the Mikkeller on Viktoria-gade, only a few minutes away. As mentioned earlier, that was the first bar Mikkel Bjergsø opened back in 2010. Today, there are over

Since Mikkeller Running Club was established in 2014, it has grown so large that around 20,000 runners, more or less, are now affiliated.

First Saturday is held every month in all chapters of the Mikkeller Running Club: here, in front of WarPigs in Copenhagen, where the running club's president, Søren Runge, is about to give a speech.

fifty bars, restaurants, and bottle shops all over the world. Most are located in Copenhagen, and for the annual Mikkellerthon, participating runners must pass by all of Mikkeller's locations along the way and imbibe a new drink at each one. Last time that came to a total of 15 kilometers—and roughly the same amount of alcohol.

"Mikkel and I wound up cheating," admits Runge. "We broke off from the group and sailed over near Nyhavn. We made a long, impromptu stop at Borgerkroen, where we sat and sang and got plastered. That said, many of the runners with us today are actually pretty serious about their races. They aren't here just to drink beer."

When Mikkel Bjergsø's sister-in-law challenged him to run a half-marathon a little over ten years ago, he was certain that he could do so easily. True, he hadn't completed one in a long time—and a good fifteen years had passed without much exercise—but he was a former elite runner, after all. That's why he was rather shellshocked when he felt so bad during the race that he had to drop out entirely—the worst possible defeat. He simply had to face the fact that he'd become too fat and inactive.

That just didn't jive with his sense of self. Back in 1986, as an eleven-year-old, he started playing sports, which quickly became serious. Only a few years later, he completed his first half-marathon with a time of 1 hour, 17 minutes, and 35 seconds. He discovered that he had the talent to tear up the asphalt. Bjergsø started getting up at five o'clock every day to run 10 kilometers, whether it was raining or snowing. He avoided alcohol, trained twelve times a week, and logged around 300–400 kilometers a month. This brought him to the attention of Danish national coach Henrik Larsen, a man of the old school, whose best advice was: "Start hard, increase along the way, and sprint at the end."

Bjergsø even became Danish champion a number of times in several different distances—but once his interest in microbrewing took off, his interest in running waned. He became a busy businessman who traveled often, ate well, and drank a lot of alcohol. The exercise that had previously filled his time basically vanished right out of his life. He did a complete turnaround: instead of being a teetotaler, he started drinking too much beer—and his body showed it. The kilos were gaining momentum now, not his feet. Before long, he weighed almost ninety kilos and started to look like the office chair he spent too much time sitting in. He became slow and lazy.

After that failed half-marathon, Bjergsø decided he needed to do something. He wasn't the only one who felt that way, either. His good friend Søren Runge found himself in a somewhat similar situation and also needed to pull it together. The two men had known each other since they were studying to become teachers; they had ended up in the same group and had gone out the first day to drink beer together. That was the start of their friendship, and they hung out a lot in the following years while both were living in the Vesterbro neighborhood in Copenhagen.

While the adolescent Bjergsø was always running, Runge had played a lot of soccer—but his active life had also come to a standstill.

"Mikkel had become very successful and was getting invitations to everything," recalls Runge. "So, he was eating well but not exercising, and he had gained a lot of weight. He got tired of himself. I'd been smoking for far too many years and had to find a way to finally quit. So, we promised each other we'd do something about it."

That was in 2013—and before long Mikkel Bjergsø's old competitive spirit had kicked back in. Just as abruptly as he had stopped, he started up again. To help motivate his friend, he promised to treat Runge to dinner at Noma if he could run a marathon in under three hours. Runge trained and trained, and even though he didn't quite make it—he burned out at 40 kilometers and came in at three hours and four minutes—he still got his well-deserved dinner.

After that, they started running more and more often. Bjergsø lost fifteen kilos in four months, and Runge—who'd been miserable trying to stop smoking—found an outlet for his anger in running. He finally quit smoking altogether. In October of 2014, they decided to invite others to join them. They created a joint Facebook page where they challenged people to show up the following Saturday and shake things up. In return, everyone would get a free beer afterwards.

Eight people showed up for the first run. When they tried it again a couple weeks later, twenty-eight people joined in. Before long, they were up to one hundred. At that time, Bjergsø had just about taken over the spaces for what later became WarPigs in the Meatpacking District. Even though it was only a construction site, they set up a keg, and soon it became their regular meeting place on the first Saturday of each month.

After some time, Bjergsø and Runge received a message from a dedicated Mikkeller fan in Sweden. He'd heard about the running club and wanted to know if he could start a similar one in Stockholm (where Mikkeller had just opened a bar). They gave him the green light. Shortly afterwards, they received another message—this time from Bangkok—and then inquiries started pouring in from near and far.

Bjergsø and Runge realized that they had something with their running club. A lot of other people enjoyed beer but also struggled with a little too much weight and a generally unhealthy lifestyle—especially in the beer industry. Therefore, the Mikkeller Running Club, as they christened it, needed to be neither exclusive nor elitist; it had to be a club for everyone who was game for a run. On the other hand, they could see that they needed to unify all of it. So, they created a manual to

"Mikkel had become very successful and was getting invitations to everything. So, he was eating well but not exercising, and he had gained a lot of weight. He got tired of himself. I'd been smoking for far too many years and had to find a way to finally quit. So we promised each other we'd do something about it."

– Søren Runge

send around every time a new chapter of the running club sprang up somewhere.

"We decided that they needed to find a clubhouse—that is, a bar—that would agree to provide the first beer for free, one Saturday each month. In return, the bar would be mentioned on social media and acquire happy new customers, so it was a win-win for everyone," explains Runge.

If they couldn't find a bar with Mikkeller on tap in the town in question, they saw to it that a tap was set up there. They also sent running shirts featuring their logo to the various clubs, so they'd have a little advertisement on the streets. After half a year, Mikkeller Running Club had grown so large that Bjergsø no longer had time to get involved in

Left: Mikkel Bjergsø at DHL, the world's largest relay race, in Fælledparken. Mikkeller participates every year.

At right: Søren Runge and Mikkel Bjergsø.

all the practicalities. Runge took over responsibility for directing the fun and games by answering inquiries and coordinating everything on social media. In addition to his job as a schoolteacher in Rødovre, he was employed to work with the running club once a week at Mikkeller's head office, located at that time on Vesterbrogade. Bjergsø then introduced a new competitive element: if the running club could hit a hundred chapters, the two friends would travel around the world to visit some of them. By 2015, they reached that goal—and Runge moved from a part-time to a full-time employee with the honorary title of President of Mikkeller Running Club.

"Mikkel always says that I have the world's coolest job," admits Runge, "because all I have to do is run and drink beer."

Before long, Mikkeller Running Club numbered 200 chapters, and then 250 chapters. They were receiving messages from such diverse places as Reykjavik, Siberia, Cape Town, Taipei, Prague, São Paulo, and Philadelphia. To create some cohesion across international borders, Runge and Bjergsø set up a very basic principle that would function as a kind of global guideline: "Enjoy life, but don't forget to train; play your sport, but remember to enjoy life."

Although Bjergsø's never intended to create a worldwide running club, that's exactly what happened. Early on, he realized that the club offered a unique opportunity to spread the Mikkeller brand and to reach target groups other than those he normally would—which was exactly what he wanted. Right from the start, Bjergsø vowed that he would not pay money to market Mikkeller. First of all, he was convinced that paid advertising would eventually fade and that maintaining quality was the best way to ensure their good reputation. If his product weren't good enough in and of itself, he didn't want to sell it. It needed to sell itself, not be stuffed down consumers' throats against their will.

Second, he was a trained schoolteacher, and his longtime right-hand man, Jacob Alsing, had been an officer in the Danish army; they weren't inclined to follow traditional marketing models. Because neither of them had any background in business theory, they had to constantly find their own way. They took their cue from the music industry. Instead of paying for marketing, they produced lots of content that could be used in the company's organic feed. Their motto was that people became better customers when they discovered things for themselves—like discovering a band that you really like, one that might even become part of your identity.

To make direct contact with Mikkeller's growing following, they utilized social media before its use had become as widespread as it is today. For example, they deliberately tried to give people the impression that the microbrewery was actually smaller than it was, to create more personal and down-to-earth contact. As a trained journalist, Pernille Pang was particularly aware, early on, that Bjergsø's own story was a central and fascinating part of Mikkeller's basic narrative. People wanted to know more about this schoolteacher who'd become an international brewer. That created a lot of attention, and they knew how to constantly breathe new life into it. When Mikkeller released Beer Geek Brunch Weasel—the beer made with coffee beans that had passed through a weasel—it quickly found fame on social media as that "shitty beer."

Even though Bjergsø was opposed to using traditional marketing techniques, he still recognized the power of merchandising in running a business. Before long, people were able to buy the brewery's T-shirts in and around the bars. That actually happened somewhat by accident when Mikkeller printed up T-shirts for the volunteers who helped pour beer at the official Danish beer festival in 2006. Some of the guests suddenly started showing an interest in buying something similar.

"Again, it's a lot like the music industry, where you have idols whom people follow and therefore buy 'merch.' There are many today who walk around in brewery T-shirts because they are fans of certain brewers, just as they are of certain bands," Bjergsø says.

As a nomadic brewery with only modest expenses for many years, Mikkeller could take far more risks than most other small Danish breweries. That gave the company more creative freedom with branding. In a constant search for what that might also encompass, the company's numerous projects and collaborations became both products in themselves and marketing tools in general. When the bar in Viktoriagade opened, it had roughly two purposes: one was, of course, to make money, but at the same time the bar also served as an extremely effective marketing platform. It was highly unusual for microbreweries to have their own bar. Instead, they wanted their beer represented at different bars—but now here was "Mikkeller" on the façade of a bar in the middle of Copenhagen.

Perhaps the best marketing stunt of all has proven to be the running club, which has given Mikkeller a reputation as a versatile brand. In addition, thousands of people around the world are now running around with the company's logos on their clothes.

"My intention wasn't to start a large business just to make money," explains Bjergsø. "It's nice to make money, but that wasn't the point. I wanted to create something bold and unique that hadn't been seen before. I wanted to put beer in a new setting and do everything differently than what the beer world was doing. That's one of the reasons why it has become so successful."

Although Mikkeller Running Club garnered a lot of interest around 2015, not everyone in the Danish running scene was equally impressed. The established running clubs began to lose some of their joggers, because

suddenly there was a running club that wasn't only free—it was also handing out free beers. At the same time, some voices in the industry were skeptical about the very concept of combining running and beer. Therefore, it became a sport in itself for Bjergsø and Runge to disprove them. The following year, for example, they competed in the Copenhagen Marathon and drank only beer. It was mid-May and temperatures had reached 25 degrees.

"Mikkel got bad cramps halfway through and had to drop out after twenty-eight kilometers," recalls Rung, "and I barely made it to the finish line. But we had to prove that it could be done, in one way or another."

Since then, Mikkeller has brewed beer specifically aimed at running—both light IPAs and their non-alcoholic Energibajer (Energy Beer). In general, one of Mikkeller Running Club's central goals is to prove that there's no real conflict between exercise and beer. To Bjergsø and Runge, there'd been too much of one or the other: people were either so serious that they wouldn't even drink a glass of wine or so lazy that they'd never exercise.

"We wanted to create a culture where it's super cool both to enjoy beer and to exercise," says Runge. "We've traveled all over the world, and we meet people who feel the same way everywhere we go. They like to drink beer and have fun, but they also know that you have to remember to get a little exercise, so you don't end up dissatisfied with yourself."

When the Great Wall Marathon was held in China in 2018, Mikkeller sponsored beer at the finish line. The company has also frequently organized the World Beer Run, in the small Portuguese town of Caminha, where Artbeerfest is held every year. Participants run ten kilometers and drink two beers along the way and plenty when they finish. In connection with the annual Mikkeller Beer Celebration, there are also various running competitions, including the famous (and infamous) Beer Mile competition, in which participants run 1,600

226   XIII. Fat and Lazy

Today, Mikkeller Running Club is represented all over the world. From top left: Copenhagen. Berlin Half-Marathon. Liverpool. Minsk. London. Moscow. Orange County.

meters and drink four beers along the way. That one requires being a good runner and a good beer drinker if people want to win, which many do, because in recent years it has become a serious discipline with a website and official records. Among other events, European championships have been held at *Østerbro* Stadium in Copenhagen. Many practice in advance with, for example, soda water to get both their throats and their stomachs accustomed to the carbonated intake. Sweden even has a national team participating in Beer Mile, which Mikkeller has long since sponsored. Bjergsø's personal record is about six minutes—about one and a half minutes slower than the world record of four minutes and thirty-three seconds.

A couple of years ago, Mikkeller Running Club launched a new app that tracked your run, as do most running apps, but this one also tracked your beer intake. If someone had either drunk too little or run too little, a scale would tilt and then send a message: "Drink more beer" or "Run more." Wherever you were in the world, you could also find the location of the nearest "clubhouse." For many members of the running club, taking their running shoes with them and joining the local chapter on a run have become a permanent part of traveling abroad. Currently there are about 200 chapters. That number fluctuates slightly, but in general the club has been widely represented worldwide for some years now. There's a chapter in Novosibirsk, for example, and at one point there was one in Joshua Tree, in the Mojave Desert in the United States. Admittedly, that one had only one member. When he eventually moved to Taipei, he had to close it down—only to open a new one in the Taiwanese capital.

Late that afternoon, a number of people are still gathered in front of WarPigs in Copenhagen. They stand around in small groups holding fresh provisions. Several have tattoos with the Mikkeller Running Club logo sticking out

from a sleeve or from the bottom of their running shorts. From strollers, wee ones follow the course of events—some are actually the result of the running club, as several members have also married along the way. For many, the club has become a focal point in their everyday life. Some started coming to training because they liked to run and then learned about microbrewing; for others, it went the other way. Common to most of them, however, is that the importance of running only grew over the years.

Once Bjergsø started running again, he realized just how much he had missed it. He had a hard time understanding how he'd done without it. Bjergsø believes that playing sports makes him both a better person and a better father—they provide a haven to help him disconnect from his busy everyday life, one where he doesn't have to think about or talk to people. Before long, he set up three treadmills in the training room with the large windows at the company's head office. Employees were free to use the room during the day. It also became a tradition that all employees were supposed to run on Wednesdays. However, the company dropped that tradition rather quickly, because not everyone was interested. Instead, today there's a running team that meets every Thursday morning—for those who want to run.

For both Bjergsø and Runge, however, their own interest developed quickly after they founded the running club. Both men started running more frequently—and competing, in several Danish Championships, for example. Others in the milieu surrounding Mikkeller Running Club had ambitions too, but they didn't want to break with the original vision for the running club. Instead, they created an alternative, the Hechmann Mikkeller Racing Club, in collaboration with renowned Danish running coach Claus Hechmann. Intended for more competitive and ambitious runners, the club's main goal was to become

Denmark's fastest running club and to win championships. They acquired various sponsorships, including Audi, and attracted several strong runners on contracts while the project was still going on. Since then, Bjergsø has also been involved in creating the running brand Final Gravity in collaboration with the design firm Femmes Régionales. The brand's name refers to the relative density of beer in relation to water.

Although Mikkeller Running Club met opposition from the organized sports world, it eventually managed to overcome the underlying skepticism. Any concerns were finally put to rest in 2018 when the Danish Athletics Association named Mikkeller its title sponsor, and the World Cup in Cross-Country was held on Danish soil. The event is one of the biggest running tournaments in the world.

"It was totally unbelievable that a brewery was allowed to sponsor it," says Bjergsø. "When we started the running club, no one had ever been able to take alcohol into events that way. It proved that we really had changed something in that world. That was really cool, because it was like a childhood dream for me—now that I couldn't become the best runner in the world."

Today, the running club is one of the accomplishments Bjergsø is most proud of, because it has helped to put focus on exercise and personal well-being in an industry not usually known for that. He can't even count how many times he has run with overweight people around the world who would never have started exercising if it weren't for Mikkeller Running Club.

"Personally, I think it's amazing to know you've made a difference, besides just making some beers."

"Personally, I think it's really cool to have made a difference beyond just making beers."

– Mikkel Bjergsø

Mikkeller Running Club's motto is that you must remember to both enjoy yourself and keep in shape—so beer and running go well together.

XIV

A NEW ERA

The daily routine is in full swing at Mikkeller's main office in Vesterbro in Copenhagen. Just inside the door on the third floor of Humletorvet in the Carlsberg district, a handful of employees have gathered on some sofas. They have an unobstructed view of the refrigerator, which is packed with microbrews, and the rust-colored bar, fully equipped with five taps and all kinds of glasses, ready for customers, business partners, and the next Friday happy hour. On this late summer day in 2021, however, there's greater demand for tea bags and coffee, the latter of which is ground near the black back wall in the kitchen. A single employee has momentarily sat down on one of the blue chairs by the long wooden table. Overhead hang a series of small blue Verner Panton lamps. The iconic designer's colorful universe forms a common thread throughout the office, where nostalgic memorabilia from Mikkeller's first bar on Viktoriagade also plays a significant role. Meetings are held in one of the small, intimate meeting rooms with their large glass façades, but the vast majority of employees sit on black office chairs at white desks next to large green potted plants in the open office.

Most of them have just returned from their summer vacation—as has Mikkel Bjergsø a few days earlier, following a week on Bornholm with Pernille Pang and their two daughters. They were "glamping," as they call it, out on a field next to a bird sanctuary. In the mornings they were awakened by roosters crowing and geese screaming as deer and hares pranced about.

"It was fucking cool," he says, "almost like a Danish safari."

The vacation was a perfect fit, as Bjergsø is currently in the process of getting his hunting license. Because he knows the animals now, he's starting to enjoy getting out there—and he's seeing them in an entirely different way. It's something he has wanted for a long time. A few years ago, he actually received a hunting license course as a birthday present, but never got to take it because time was too tight. He's finally found the time now.

"It's nice just to get out in nature and relax. That's really what I'm doing it for—it's a way of getting out there and not thinking about anything."

At the end of 2020, Mikkel Bjergsø announced that he had chosen to step down as CEO of Mikkeller. Instead, Kenneth Madsen, former head of the jewelry company Pandora in Asia and Australia, would become the company's new managing director. Madsen had started his career in the Danish brewing giant Carlsberg twenty-five years earlier; he was also employed by both EMI Capitol Music and ECCO Shoes, and subsequently spent seven years in Hong Kong as head of Pandora. Bjergsø was involved in selecting his replacement for the top position in the company that he had built up from scratch. Because Mikkeller had grown so much in recent years, he'd become too ensconced in administrative work. By turning over the reins, he could seize the opportunity to concentrate on the part he's best at and likes most—product development and branding—in his new role as creative director.

Bjergsø had decided to hire a new CEO about a year and a half earlier when he was starting to feel alone at the top. He had acknowledged that, basically, he didn't even have the qualifications for the role. He had steered the ship as far as he could, but the company had simply become too large. He was constantly aware of his own limitations. Someone else was needed to add more structure to everything if it was going to last.

Bjergsø had actually been ruminating about resigning as CEO of Mikkeller for a much longer period of time. For too many years he'd spent most of his time working on something that he didn't really think was exciting. He often thought it was a waste of his time to expend energy on something others could do better. In the company's infancy, he did all of it on his own: the bookkeeping, accounts, and tax returns. His interests lay elsewhere, but he had to do all of it, because Mikkeller was a one-man army. Later, when there were more employees, more hands came on board. Yet, at the same time, the amount of administration work also increased. Far too often, he found himself sitting in meetings and talking about budgets. When the investment firm Orkila Capital entered the picture in 2016—and business really took off—reports suddenly had to be delivered all the time about one thing and another.

"I'd never dreamed of becoming the managing director of a company," admits Bjergsø. "It was something that just happened, because I started something that ended up growing. But my strength isn't sitting at board meetings or drawing up budgets. I can easily figure it out, but my time is better spent developing projects. It's something I'd been thinking about for a long time, and I should probably have done it sooner. But time passes when you're busy."

For many years Mikkeller was Mikkel and Mikkel was Mikkeller. That the brand had become so identified with its founder was both a gift and a curse. The press found him intriguing, and people expected him to appear at all the openings around the world. He became the "giraffe" people came to see. As the company grew, however, he began to feel the pressure of always having to be everywhere.

For a couple of years, he thought every day about stopping as chief executive. The problem was that he still wanted control. Bjergsø found it unnatural to relinquish responsibility, because then he risked being replaced by someone who wasn't as dedicated—and what would be the consequences?

"It's hard to give up the responsibility," explains Bjergsø, "if you don't feel that those taking over the responsibility can do the job the same way that I'd do it. That *is* hard, but maybe it really shouldn't be easy anyway.

I actually don't think that it's ever easy for someone who starts his own business … maybe I've just been exceptionally bad at letting go."

Because being annoyed all the time was taking a toll on him, Pernille Pang tried repeatedly to explain to Bjergsø that he had to accept the fact that others don't have the same drive—but that was easier said than done. He'd grown up in a state of constant competition with his twin brother. It was ingrained in him that he always had to be first and best at everything; otherwise, someone else would be. That was why he needed constant control and perfectionism, and that was why he had a hard time accepting it when things weren't done exactly the way he wanted them.

"It's seriously stressful when everything has to be perfect and exactly the way I want it. I've been unable to sleep at night for many years, but I don't think I can change that either. That's just the person I am. Nothing in my life is random."

Ever since Bjergsø discovered the world of microbrewing in the early 2000s, he's been convinced that he'd probably never completely stop making beer again (even though he's fantasized about buying a deserted wine castle and making wine instead). On the other hand, he's known for a long time that he shouldn't sit on the same post for the next thirty years—for his own good and for Mikkeller's.

For many years, Bjergsø had to travel frequently, so time with his family was limited. He was self-employed, however, and when you run your own business, you're on all the time. You can't just pull the plug for fourteen days to go on vacation. There was always something that needed fixing or some small fires to put out. Mostly, his inner drive kept pushing him forward, forward, forward.

For Pang, that meant she often found herself alone with the children, even when they were still quite young. For a long time, she thought that she just couldn't change

him—that his inner restlessness compelled him to go out into the world and create something. After being together for over twenty years, however, the gaps in their relationship grew even deeper, and in 2019 they separated. Because they were both children of divorce who'd experienced their parents' bad breakups and subsequent bad relationships, they were keen on doing things differently. Now that they were the ones divorcing, they wanted to maintain a positive and loving relationship. They had been a loyal unit for many years—at Mikkeller, as well—and they continued to be one. For them, continuing to work closely turned out to be surprisingly uncomplicated—maybe because they insisted on making it uncomplicated.

After a couple eventful years, Bjergsø has been able to relax more, possibly for the first time in his life. He realizes that there are better ways to expend your energy than wondering if your kitchen cabinets really match. Even he thinks it's because he's getting older. He has also learned a lot from having children, however, and watching them grow to become small, independent people.

"There are plenty of things about children that aren't perfect," he observes, "and you have to accept a crazy number of things you'd never accept in yourself. That has put some things in relief. At the same time, I've been working so hard for so many years now on something that had to be exactly as I wanted it to be that I think I've just become exhausted."

At times Bjergsø can almost completely let go of his inner need for control—but then it suddenly returns. Typically, he'll have a few days where he becomes annoyed with everything in the company: "Why was this done this way? And why wasn't it done like this?" Therefore, finding a new managing director with a lot of experience who is far more professionally trained for the role has been healthy for Bjergsø on a personal level. It has allowed him to let go of some of that control.

"It couldn't go on like that, with me wanting to control everything. It's probably a good thing that I've recognized that—well, at least to some extent. Eighty percent of me has admitted that I might as well let it go, because I can't control all of it anyway."

With only only a week to go before the Mikkeller Beer Celebration in the fall of 2021, everything suddenly started to fall apart. Several of the invited breweries—especially the American and Canadian—announced they were canceling, one after the other, in response to criticism of Mikkeller that was created by voices on Instagram earlier that year and that only grew in strength. It became one of the bigger stories in the media that the company was experiencing challenges because of its unhealthy work culture. Suddenly, Mikkeller became a brand some of the festival's participating breweries didn't want to be associated with. A total of 39 microbreweries announced that they wouldn't be participating in the festival that had, in many ways, become the company's landmark. If there ever was a time when Bjergsø had to admit that it's impossible to have control over everything, that was it. Now the very story of Mikkeller was suddenly slipping out of his hands.

The whole unfortunate affair had its origins in the spring of the same year, when a female brewer and production manager in Massachusetts posted a message on Instagram asking if anyone else in the brewing industry had experienced sexism. A series of reports streamed in from breweries around the world, including Mikkeller, where initially anonymous respondents reported bullying, harassment, and an unsafe environment. The stories revolved around Mikkeller's brewery in San Diego and WarPigs in Copenhagen. Although Bjergsø wasn't in the direct line of fire for any accusations, the underlying message was that he and the rest of upper management in Mikkeller had turned a blind eye to it.

A sign at Mikkeller's brewpub WarPigs signals focus on both diversity and inclusion within the company.

Bjergsø had a hard time recognizing that accusation. Over the years, he had frequently reprimanded or even fired people who weren't behaving properly. He was well aware, therefore, that there had been cases of that nature when they first saw the light of day. On the other hand, Bjergsø was also of the opinion that they'd already been handled.

"I had kicked people right out of the company for doing stupid things," explains Bjergsø. "I've always had a heightened sense of justice. I hate when people don't behave properly—it drives me totally crazy. So, it also felt really extreme to suddenly be standing in the line of fire for things I couldn't even recognize. Mikkeller's set of values has always been very important to me, something I've been really proud of. Suddenly we were being portrayed as a company with a toxic culture. It felt like an unfair attack."

Not everyone saw it that way, however. During the summer of 2021, criticism began to increase—and that fall, as the Mikkeller Beer Celebration was approaching, it really took off. Mikkeller found itself in the middle of a shitstorm, and upper management had split into two wings: those who wanted to take it lying down and those who thought they needed to retaliate. Bjergsø belonged to the latter group. In an interview with the Danish radio station P1, he rejected the notion of broad cultural problems in Mikkeller, and in the newspaper *Berlingske*, he accused critics of being online activists trying to destroy his business by putting pressure on breweries to force them to drop out of the festival.

"I've always been a person who speaks his mind," insists Bjergsø. "I've often been criticized for it—but I find it difficult to say something that goes against what I really believe just because people want to hear it. If I think things are unfair or have been done incorrectly, then I say so. I'm never going to take my opponent's position just to keep the peace."

The next day, both radio and newspaper interviews were translated into English and surfaced all over social media. That didn't exactly alleviate the criticism. Instead, the company's new CEO, Kenneth Madsen, appeared in the press, where he did an about-face and apologized for the frequent episodes. He promised to initiate a major clean-up to ensure a better and safer culture going forward. A few days later, Bjergsø also apologized on Instagram: "We should have been more pro-active in preventing what has happened. We've acted too late and too little. I am very sorry for the interview I gave to *Berlingske*, which left the impression that I don't recognize the company's responsibility."

The negative stories left their mark on the head office in Copenhagen. No peace would be had until Bjergsø showed up at a townhall meeting and, clearly moved, spoke about how sorry he was about the situation and what should have been handled differently. Subsequently, both Bjergsø and Pang had conversations with employees who needed them. Meanwhile, management at Mikkeller continued to analyze everything that had happened in the company's approximately fifteen-year history, when over two thousand people had been employed at over fifty bars and restaurants. In hindsight, there might have been too much of a rock'n'roll vibe in the company. People felt like they could walk on water just because they were successful and everyone wanted to work there. Therefore, a kind of "if you can't take the heat, get out of the kitchen" attitude might have unconsciously crept into the workplace. If someone became dissatisfied, the company had no problem finding someone else.

At the same time, the company lacked the structure or any process to take care of the issues that would inevitably arise. In a way, it was the classic story of a small business that grows larger yet continues to do most things the same way. There was no human resources department at Mikkeller, for example, because no one in the company had any experience in it. For a long time, the company was run by friends and acquaintances; virtually all employees were hired because of their passion—not because they were trained to think corporately. That became a particular problem after Orkila Capital came on board and business really took off. Several of the leading figures were overwhelmed by their workload. They no longer had time to be everywhere at once or get a sense of employees' moods. If workers experienced problems with harassment or a poor work environment, they had to go to either Mikkel Bjergsø or Jacob Alsing—and that was problematic for obvious reasons. The company lacked the necessary intermediaries.

The ensuing time involved a painful process of self-awareness for Bjergsø, who was forced to admit that something had been beyond his control. As a control freak and perfectionist, he had a hard time accepting it. Because Mikkeller had been so keen on putting out fires and dismissing the image of the company that had been presented—one they didn't recognize—they'd failed to listen to the people who felt that they'd been subjected to harassment and bullying.

"In retrospect, there'd been too little focus on that part of running a business," observes Bjergsø. "I think it's a typical phenomenon for a small business that grows but then forgets to create a professional framework. I wish I could have done things differently. Unfortunately, you often find out about something like this only when problems start to surface."

Earlier in 2022, Mikkeller announced that it had launched a "reconciliation program" in collaboration with Kate Bailey, founder and managing director of Hand & Heart Business Consulting, who had been at the forefront of criticism of the company's work culture. The company's goal was to take care of those who'd had negative experiences. In addition, management has maintained a strong focus on ensuring that in the future Mikkeller will be totally prepared to handle these sorts of incidents. To put it another way, the company will be equipped to take Bjergsø's ever-growing brainchild the last step toward becoming a truly professional organization.

"We have about six or seven hundred employees all over the world," explains Bjergsø, "in an industry involving alcohol and night hours, so it's completely impossible to guarantee that nothing will ever happen in the future. Some manager might step out of line or some customer might behave unacceptably. On the other hand, we can guarantee that in the future we'll have a completely different process in place to handle it in the best possible way. On that front, we've come a long way in a short time and have learned an incredible amount—the hard way."

XV

TOWARD OTHER GOALS

– DRAFT –

KRIEK VANILJE	WILD ALE w/ CHERRIES, CINNAMON & VANILLA		7%	70	20 cl.
VIOLET BEVERAGE	WILD ALE w/ ROXEN BERRIES		7%	70	20 cl.
EARS OF PLENTY	RUSTIC DANISH WHEAT SAISON		7%	60	20 cl.
STEVNSBÆR #2	DANISH WILD ALE AGED ON CHERRIES		8,1%	70	20 cl.
RUUD PEESCH	DANISH WILD ALE AGED ON RED VINEYARD PEACHES		6%	70	20 cl.
I WOULD NOT FEEL SO ALL ALONE #2	DANISH WILD ALE AGED WITH PEACHES AND APRICOTS		6,5%	70	20 cl.
N NORDLUNDS FIELD BLEND #2	DANISH WILD ALE AGED ON WINE & TABLE GRAPES		8,8%	70	20 cl.
N HAVNESÆSON	OAK-AGED RUSTIC DANISH SAISON		7,2%	70	20 cl.
EN REF SÆ SØEN ABRIKOS	DANISH SAISON W/ APRICOT		6,5%	70	20 cl.
...LER SIDE EYES	PALE ALE		4,6%	35/65	
...LER JACKIE BROWN	BROWN ALE		6%	35/65	
...LER ORG. GERMAN PILS	PILS		5%	30/55	
...LER WIT	BELGIAN WHEAT ALE		4,5%	30/55	
...ERIE DE LA SENNE TARAS BOULBA	BELGIAN BLONDE		4,5%	60/40 cl.	
...LER HEATED SEATS	N.E.IPA		4,9%	35/85	
...LER BEER GEEK RIESLING	WHITE WINE (not beer)		11%	75	12

Tickets available now!

- BLUE SESSION: Friday (17-21.00)
- RED SESSION: early Saturday (12-16.00)
- GREEN SESSION: late Saturday (17-21.00)
- ORANGE SESSION: all Saturday (12-21.00)

... AND MORE!

The Mikkeller Baghaven Wild Ale Festival will bring some of the premier producers of spontaneous, wild, and mixed fermentation beers from around the world.

We will gather in Copenhagen, DK, to showcase some of the finest and most exclusive wild beers being produced today.

⦿ wildale.celebration2020
f wildalecelebration

MIKKELLER BAGHAVEN WILD ALE CELEBRATION

2020
M.B.W.A.C
7-8 feb

OXBOW
CASEY
Lindema...
BURNING SKY
BOKKE
BOO...
HILL FARMS BREW...
De Garde
Œ R...
2nd SHIF...
Jester King

ORVAL

One Tuesday morning in August of 2022, the company announced that Kenneth Madsen would step down as CEO—fewer than two years after he joined with the intent of expanding business into untapped markets. Instead, Mikkeller would introduce a new management team consisting of the company's finance manager, Martin Connie Pinborg, chief legal officer and forewoman of the board, Ditte Lassen-Kahlke, and Mikkel Bjergsø, who would take care of day-to-day management in cooperation with a management team. The company also announced that it was scrapping its expansive business strategy to focus more on "strengthening work in branding and innovation."

To outsiders, it might have seemed strange that the company suddenly changed its strategy, but the current world situation had forced Mikkeller to abandon its plans to grow. Instead, they would be reducing costs to the bare minimum. Therefore, Kenneth Madsen was no longer the right CEO, as Mikkel Bjergsø explained it that same Tuesday morning:

"When Kenneth was hired two years ago, we were planning to expand. After two years of the pandemic and a war in Ukraine, we find ourselves in a whole new situation. With shipping costs, a shortage of raw materials, and one thing or another, everything has become more expensive and more difficult. So we agreed to part ways here. The whole world is shit right now, so it doesn't make sense to be talking about growth and expansion."

Entering 2022, Mikkeller was a completely different company than it had been only a few years earlier in terms of reputation, structure, and size. In the past, people were hired simply because they had some relationship to the company—and sometimes it became clear that they were underqualified once the job became more demanding. Those people were replaced along the way, and today Mikkeller is dominated by other profiles with a completely different level of professionalism.

With its corporate structure and a professional team at its helm, Mikkeller became a company that was primarily profit-oriented. Previously, Mikkeller was rebellious in its attitude, maybe even anarchist, but now it had matured, looking more like the medium-sized company it had finally turned into.

That development, which had been going on for a long time, only accelerated further after Mikkel Bjergsø stepped down and handed the reins to Kenneth Madsen. On the other hand, the change created new challenges. Bjergsø, in his new role as creative director, tried to preserve the company's original identity, but he and Madsen didn't always understand each other. While Bjergsø is self-taught and not professionally trained in running a business—he has always simply followed his gut—Madsen speaks fluent corporate language, which has not always been easy to reformat into something understandable to both men.

In many ways, it had turned into the classic battle between founder and business manager. Although Bjergsø had previously made decisions based solely on what he wanted, going forward Mikkeller had to think in more business-oriented terms. For example, opening bars in places like Bucharest, which had been done in the past, no longer made sense, as the people there couldn't even afford to buy the beer. Also, the company suddenly needed to keep beer in stock to maintain more of a presence in supermarkets, which meant that in the future they needed a core range of eight beers—and they'd have to sell a lot of them. That had definitely not been the case before, to put it mildly, because Bjergsø had always found core-range series incredibly dull. Instead, it had almost become his mantra to spit out new beers all the time, and once they sold out, just make new ones. Part of the company's charm was that it was moving in so many directions. Still, it didn't make much sense business-wise. Now, a plan was made instead for each individual beer, concerning where and how to market it in the wisest way.

For Bjergsø, the changes sometimes brought ugly associations with some of the original American microbreweries. According to him, they sell a lot of beer these days, but no one in the beer world finds them particularly interesting. In pursuit of selling as much as possible, you can become beer's answer to Joe & The Juice—known by everyone, loved by no one.

"Sometimes I have to swallow my pride," admitted Bjergsø in early 2022, "but we've grown. The only alternative is for me to take over the reins again—and that would not be a good idea. I have a lot of employees whose salaries I need to pay, so we can't just go around doing projects wherever the wind blows. Still, it's pretty clear that, personally, I find it difficult that we're doing things today that I would never do. Conversely, there are things I'd like to do that we don't do anymore. I accept that—there's no turning back."

Once Bjergsø took on a different role in Mikkeller, life became both liberating and, at times, a little scary. Every so often a thought reared its head in the back of his mind: Can your brainchild grow so big that that it renders you unnecessary?

"We have a CEO now who's more corporate and naturally really wants to sell beer. Besides, that's his ultimate responsibility. I offer a counterbalance, because we also have to make sure that the brand stays relevant. His whole way of thinking is completely different than mine when we started. There has to be a balance, because if I just let go of all of it, they don't need someone like me. Then I might as well just sit back and let the money roll in."

Bjergsø had no immediate plans to do that, however. Although he sometimes found the company's new conditions frustrating, he understood fully that there were other priorities now—and that it made sense to consider them if he wanted Mikkeller to go on conquering the world.

"If artists want to sell a lot of albums, they can't make music that's too wild. They have to be more mainstream. That's just the way life is. And I can't keep sending sixteen percent imperial stouts out into the world if no one's going to drink them. I really have no interest in that anyway. For many years, Mikkeller was an elitist brand for a small crowd of beer nerds who were really into beer. It was exclusive and expensive. I think it's cool to be able to offer our beer to a lot more people today," comments Bjergsø.

That's a point on which both Mikkel Bjergsø and Kenneth Madsen—despite their differences—agreed wholeheartedly: their vision to reach as many people as possible with Mikkeller's beer.

"Sometimes I lie awake at night and wonder if I should be doing something else. I've done this for so many years now. At the same time, I can see that there's still a lot more to achieve. Many people don't know us yet, and I'd really like them to drink our beer."

A few years ago, the opportunity arose for Mikkeller to collaborate with the American media group Warner Bros. on their most popular television series to date. Being an all-or-nothing-at-all person, Bjergsø had never found time to delve into movies and television series. So, even though he'd heard the name before, he had no idea whether it was of any interest to Mikkeller. Forwarding the inquiry to Pernille Pang, he asked her: "Pretty cool, don't you think?" Realizing what it was, she responded quickly: "Yes, it's a big deal …" As it turned out, Warner Bros. Consumer Products was interested in collaborating on the hugely popular HBO series *Game of Thrones*, and later the series' prequel *House of the Dragon*, which premiered in late summer 2022.

At that time, Mikkeller had only recently acquired a new CEO, Kenneth Madsen, and the timing was fortuitous. Thanks to his long career at the helm of numerous large groups, Madsen had a completely different

experience with this kind of huge collaboration in which you have to obtain myriad approvals and sign a lot of contracts concerning technicalities. Eventually, they managed to land the deal, which meant that Mikkeller would make Game of Thrones-branded beers worldwide over a multi-year period. The collaboration has already produced ten beers. "If everything goes well, it could mean a lot for our profits in the coming years," says Bjergsø. "In terms of branding, it will also mean a lot, because we'll have the potential to reach two hundred and fifty million people who didn't already know us. Because they collect Game of Thrones merchandise, they'll buy our beer and discover that there's something called Mikkeller. And if they have good experiences, they might want to buy even more from us in the future. It's totally huge—our biggest collaboration ever."

In 2021, Mikkeller became the first brewery to launch a series of official Hans Christian Andersen beers. The launch coincided with the opening of a new museum for the world-famous fairy tale poet in his hometown of Odense. For the Danish microbrewery, the project has the potential to become a kind of Trojan horse in the Chinese market, which many companies in recent years have been trying to break into. Hans Christian Andersen is enormously popular there—so if handled properly, it might make it possible to barrel into a gigantic market where specialty beers still haven't really taken hold.

"It has enormous potential in Asia, if we hit it just right," said Bjergsø about the opportunity.

Several years have passed since Bjergsø started discussing the fact that running bars in the US, for example, had almost become too easy. Therefore, he was more preoccupied with entering other, more untapped markets, where they could actually make a difference and change things. The Chinese market holds particular interest, because Mikkeller could both disseminate the good fortunes of the microbrewery to legions of people and, at the same time, access completely new, huge sources of income. With Kenneth Madsen in his new role as CEO, the company had finally found the right person to lead the beer invasion.

Although 2020 wasn't exactly the ideal time to open new bars, with the world more or less in constant lockdown, Mikkeller still managed to open its first two bars in the world's most populous country. The first, designed in a style of fusion between Scandinavian minimalism and elements of Chinese architecture, was located in Jing'an, one of the central districts of Shanghai, a ten-minute drive north of the traditional Buddhist Jing'an Temple. The area, which has become a popular beer destination in the last few years, is a perfect fit for a Mikkeller bar. However, beer sales there are still dominated by large beer brands competing in price and market share, whereas craft beer in the general population is still considered a niche product.

Less than a year later, Mikkeller opened another bar in the Chinese metropolis—this time in the Huangpu district of the fast-growing Xintiandi area. Meaning "New Heaven and Earth," Xintiandi is a pedestrian area filled with shops, restaurants, and entertainment.

Although the last few years have been unusually tough for Mikkeller—due partly to the pandemic and partly to a poor media coverage—in early 2022 there was a sense within the company that they were standing at the threshold of a whole new era. They were finally ready to expand and conquer the largest market of all.

Mikkeller has entered into an agreement with Warner Bros. Consumer Products to create a series of beers for both *Game of Thrones* and the new series *House of the Dragon*.

Sunshine by Mikkeller

For Bjergsø, personally, his greatest desire was to spearhead a change in beer culture in a part of the world where there's still a lot to do:

"I think it would be awesome if in ten years we could say that we were the ones who started it all, if I could be the pioneer. Then we'd feel we really left our mark on something."

Word came in the summer of 2022, however, that the company needed to move in another direction. Like any other brewery, Mikkeller is also affected by price increases. They have to take them seriously so they don't lose too much money selling beer. Therefore, the major goal of opening myriad new bars and restaurants and conquering even more of the world—especially the Chinese market—has been replaced with the smaller goal of becoming profitable again starting in the first quarter of 2023.

"Right now, we're losing money selling beer. We simply haven't moved fast enough, which is one of the reasons we're creating a different and flatter structure going forward— we *have* to fix that," he says.

For Bjergsø, personally, putting the company's large ambitions on hold for a while is a double-edged sword. On one hand, it's a snag in their dream of world domination, but on the other hand, it leads the Danish brewery down a more familiar path: it's not only about

Mikkeller has collaborated with the new Hans Christian Andersen Museum in Odense on a series of beers. The various labels are inspired by the fairy-tale author's paper clippings.

A label from a series of beers Mikkeller has collaborated on with the Hans Christian Andersen Museum in Odense.

growing faster and faster, but also about strengthening Mikkeller's brand.

"In recent years I've been mostly on the sidelines," comments Bjergsø. "I'm looking forward to coming back and really working with the brand again, because it *has* faded a bit into the background. For me, it's exciting to return to the 'good old days,' where everything isn't just about getting bigger."

Not that many years have passed since Mikkeller was still a beer intended only for the specially initiated. Today it's common knowledge that you can find beer from the microbrewery in many supermarkets. Naturally, this change has created challenges image-wise. Some believe that the brand's original hipster factor has been diluted—that the company has sold out its coolness for increased accessibility. Even some people at Mikkeller feel that way. Although Mikkel Bjergsø understands the criticism, a long time ago he accepted the fact that when you grow, you inevitably become less valuable in some people's eyes.

"In some ways, it's similar to the music industry," says Bjergsø. "It's the same thing there—if you get too big, people think you've sold out. If you sign with a big label, you're an asshole who makes crappy music, and then people find the next indie band to adore. That's exactly how it is in the beer industry—in some people's eyes, Carlsberg must be a bunch of bastards. I'm not like that. Of course, there's a difference between standing on a beer crate trying to get people's attention and now, when ten thousand people show up at our own festival. They're simply two different things. *Then* we can discuss which is best."

On one hand, it seems only natural to Bjergsø that the bigger you get the more difficult it becomes to maintain your brand. On the other hand, he has had to recognize, increasingly in the past few years, that Mikkeller must work hard to hold on to its current status as one of the most important craft beer brands in the world.

"It forces us to be innovative, to create interesting products beyond our eight core-range beers, which has been our focus lately. We can't just assume that people will think we're exciting. People in Mikkeller realize that we need to return to being more of a brand. That's the company's true value—that's what people buy," he explains.

For the same reason, Bjergsø chooses to view these latest developments not as a setback but as a necessary step back to return to the right course. In his own words, Bjergsø already has "lots of cool plans" for Mikkeller—plans that he's looking forward to launching and that he believes, brand-wise, will have a positive impact on business. For him, the most important thing ultimately is that the brand remains strong if in the long run he wants to succeed in getting people to drink Mikkeller beer all over the globe.

"Some people think that producing a hundred bottles that are difficult to find is automatically better than producing five hundred thousand bottles—even if it's the same beer. If you ask beer nerds, many will probably say that Mikkeller isn't as good as we were in the beginning. But that's just nonsense. We have much better opportunities to do things properly than in the old days when Keller and I were running around in that worn-out, old brewery on Funen. At the same time, I've never hidden the fact that my ambition is to get as many people as possible to drink my beer. I'd rather have seven billion people drinking them than only five hundred down on Viktoriagade."

Mikkeller
The Unusual Story of an Unusual (Beer) Brand

© 2022 Anders Ryehauge and Strandberg Publishing
Editor: Louise Haslund-Christensen
Translation: Mark Mussari
Copy-editing: Cornelius H. Colding
Image coordination: Pernille Pang
Graphic design: Spine Studio

The book is set in Agipo, Girott og Larish Alte
Paper: Tauro Offset, 140 g
Image processing: Narayana Press, Gylling
Printing and binding: Printer Trento, Italy
Printed in Italy, 2022
1st edition, 1st print run
ISBN: 978-87-94102-22-3

Strandberg Publishing A/S
Gammel Mønt 14,5
DK1117 Copenhagen K
www.strandbergpublishing.dk

THANKS

Jacob Birch
Theis Mortensen
Camilla Stephan

PHOTO CREDITS

With the exception of the following, the photos in the book belong to Mikkeller and are taken by:

Theis Mortensen, Rasmus Malmstrøm, Camilla Stephan, Søren Quvang, Neil Walton, Lars Engelgaar, Lukáš Bukoven, Magnus R. Poulsen, Danielle Adams for Becca PR og Takumi Ota.

Darren Rowlands – 175
Jasper Carlberg – 172, 214
Jeppe Carlsen – 12
Kyle Ferino – 120
Pelle Rink/Ritzau Scanpix – 49
Peter Neill – 161, 174, 177
Thomas Steen Sørensen – 41
Torben Stroyer/Jyllands-Posten/Ritzau Scanpix – 36